Baby Talk/Parent Talk

Baby Talk/ Parent Talk

Understanding Your Baby's Body Language

SIRGAY SANGER, M.D.

Photographs by Rolf Bruderer
*Produced by Alison Brown Cerier Book Development
and The Stonesong Press, Inc.*

DOUBLEDAY

NEW YORK, LONDON, TORONTO, SYDNEY, AUCKLAND

PUBLISHED BY DOUBLEDAY
a division of Bantam Doubleday Dell Publishing Group, Inc.
666 Fifth Avenue, New York, New York 10103

DOUBLEDAY and the portrayal of an anchor with a dolphin are trademarks
of Doubleday, a division of Bantam Doubleday Dell Publishing Group, Inc.

Library of Congress Cataloging-in-Publication Data

Sanger, Sirgay, 1935–
Baby talk/parent talk : Understanding your baby's body language / Sirgay
Sanger.—1st ed. in the U.S.A.

　　p.　　cm.

1. Infants.　　2. Parent and child.　　3. Infant psychology.　　4. Nonverbal
communication in infants.　　I. Title.
HQ774.S26　　1991
305.23'2—dc20　　　　　　　　　　　　　　　　　　　　　　　89-25944
　　　　　　　　　　　　　　　　　　　　　　　　　　　　　　　　CIP

ISBN 0-385-26776-2

Printed in the United States of America

January 1991

First Edition

Contents

Learning Your Baby's Signals

Your baby tells you when he wants to play and when he needs to be quietly alone. He asks to sleep, for food, for hugs. He lets you know when he's afraid, surprised, bored, fascinated, or content. He may just purr.

Babies communicate their frustrations and their joys—not with words, of course, but with their entire bodies. Babies are born with a surprisingly large repertoire of body language, which expands rapidly.

But as a parent, you may find yourself wondering what exactly your baby is trying to say. Haven't you heard yourself say in puzzlement, "What does he *want?*"

This book will help you answer that question. Through photographs, you'll learn the meaning of signals and expressions common to all babies. Some of these cues are obvious, some are subtle and easily overlooked. For example, a yawn may mean that your baby is overstimulated and trying to calm himself, not that he is ready for a nap. Some signals are misinterpreted. You might think your one-month-old is angry at you, whereas he'll need three months more to achieve focused anger.

At my Early Care Center in New York, I have helped parents like you pick up their babies' signs more accurately, consistently, and confidently. The center is the first private facility in the United States devoted exclusively to the emotional and social well-being of healthy infants and families. I have been privileged to work with hundreds of parents who deeply care about connecting with their babies' feelings. Some have a special concern—perhaps their baby is easily overstimulated, or has colic, or was born prematurely. Most just want to understand and love their babies more perceptively.

Through meeting babies and their parents, then videotaping for closer observation, I've learned the many ways in which thoughts and feelings are expressed. My conclusions have been supported by the work of other developmental psychiatrists and psychologists who have been researching baby body language over the last decade.

Together parents and I review their videotapes at the Early Care Center; they learn how much they already know about their babies' signals, although they may not realize it. We celebrate the successful exchanges parents have had, and I describe how many more are possible. Parenting needs nourishment. From time to time, you can doubt your connection with your infant. Were you then to feel embarrassed, nervous, or guilty, in communicating with your baby, this could disturb your family's natural harmony. At such times, you need to know the signals to look for and which signals to send.

Why It's Important to Learn Baby Talk

For many reasons, you'll need to become the best "baby reader" you can be. By reflecting your baby's feelings, you affirm who she is in a deep and lasting way. This feedback is so vital to infants that mirroring their actions will start a friendship. They love to be validated even in this simple way. To make them feel recognized and accepted requires your understanding the deeper meanings of their signals.

Furthermore, what you choose to ignore or highlight greatly influences your baby's emotional development. If you consistently react positively or negatively, or ignore, a signal, your baby will come to anticipate your reaction. Your feedback helps your baby organize her feelings. It also helps her to know which behavior is acceptable and unacceptable in your family.

As you respond to your baby, and she in turn remembers how you responded, she learns to moderate her emotional extremes. It's equally unhelpful to ignore as it is to overreact to your baby's pain, sadness, or anger. By watching her cues, you can keep yourself in balance and help your baby learn to regulate her feelings. She'll move beyond all-or-nothing reacting sooner and learn to respond in more appropriate and variably delightful ways.

Your baby's cues actually change under your influence. For example, two-year-olds are happier when mothers respond more quickly to their need for quiet in the first year. Also there is less lip compression (a signal of control of anger) when mothers react to anger with compassion rather than with surprise. Infants smile less when they are not in tune with their caregivers. And a fast, appropriate response to crying leads directly to less crying.

Your baby's signals are asking you to help her reestablish her harmony. Perhaps she's irritable during a feeding. Her toy might have fallen off or you might be feeding her too quickly. The emotional cue is for two people's benefit—the baby marks her own need and gets you to do something that will allow her to feel secure again. If she's scared, her fear pinpoints the danger so you can remove or avoid it. Fear lets you know how to protect her. Joy signals you to continue what you both are doing to maintain a positive balance and an optimistic mood.

As you become more attuned to your baby, you'll be able to pick up her signals earlier. You'll easily see and hear the early warning signs rather than have to wait for tears. You'll learn when your baby is becoming overstimulated so you can let her regain her balance. Your competence will have enabled her to do this for herself by the time she's two.

Responding to your baby's signals is a back-and-forth, turn-taking activity. As you learn to read your baby, you'll know when she's ready to take in information, when she's busy informing herself, and when she's reflecting on what she's just learned. So you'll know who's "got the ball." Taking turns—speaking then listening, acting then relaxing—is the precursor of conversation.

Reading your baby will help her affirm her sense of self and develop the ability to regulate emotional extremes. Responding earlier to the direction of her mood and meeting her needs more completely teaches her the value of participating in "conversation."

But don't expect your baby to say "thank you" for your efforts. In fact, if you're in close communication with your baby, she will hardly notice you. A glance now and then, a few playful interchanges while you supply a diaper or a toy, and she's off again. She checks you out to confirm safety, danger, or the mastery of a new task. As the months go by, your baby won't need to study your face and voice as much because you've become a presence inside her. You're a useful, trusted inner companion.

The Approach and Avoid Cues

The best time to get to know your baby is when he is quietly alert. While relaxed and attentive, he can best learn about himself, you, and the world.

To help your baby attain this receptive condition, you need to become an astute observer of his "engagement" and "disengagement" cues. These tell you when the baby is ready or open to your teaching and warmth, and when he wants to avoid stimulation and take a break. Withdrawal signs are more vigorous than those of engagement because they result from overly intense stimulation and are more dramatic physically. Signals to maintain moderately stimulating, pleasant experiences are less urgent and tend to be seen in only one part of the body at a time. Every infant has his own repertoire of engagement and disengagement signals.

Learning your baby's early disengagement cues will help you anticipate and avoid the buildup of intense negative emotions, which are more difficult to manage. Your baby may signal a need for a break with a snore, sneeze, yawn, hiccups, increased sucking noises, or a whimper. If he shows no facial expression, looks tired or perhaps closes his eyes partly, this is called "sobering." Another mild signal is the "ugh" expression, a wrinkled nose and slightly raised upper lip. Sometimes you'll see a pout or a slight protruding of the tongue. He may also signal that a break is needed by turning his eyes away from you or an object. His eyes may blink, flutter, or shut tightly. Sometimes he will press his lips together while rolling them in, or show his teeth while grimacing with the corners of his mouth pulled back.

Your baby can use his body to show signs of disengagement, too. One sign is when he brings his lower arms closely over his stomach and allows his hands to flail about. Other body movements include arms straightened out along the sides, shrugged shoulders, legs held straight and stiff, kicking legs, or any increased foot movement. Overall immobility or jerky and stiff movements of the arms and legs are early signals of an infant's need for a rest from interaction. Sometimes an infant will use his hands to show you that he needs a pause. You can see this when your baby holds his own hand, puts his hand on the back of his neck or behind his head, puts his hand on his mouth or stomach, or puts his hand to his ear. The fingers and wrist can be even more subtle indicators of your baby's desire to interrupt the action. For example, one or more fingers straightened or hyperextended is a disengagement signal. Similarly, some early cues that your baby needs a break are when he quickly rotates, flexes, or extends his wrists.

Strong disengagement cues include three types of crying: hunger, anger, and pain. You can usually recognize a hunger cry because it is quieter than most and consists of one or two second vocalizations with pauses in between. The cries and pauses alternate in a regular rhythm. The anger cry is basically a more forceful version of the hunger cry, but it still has an even rhythm. The pain cry is loud and sudden and lasts about seven seconds. Then the baby audibly breathes out, gulps in some more air, and starts over again. A baby of one month may show a need for a lull by merely making a crying face, without actually crying. Babies under one month will sometimes go from alertness to sleep when they need to withdraw. Choking or vomiting are also clear disengagement cues.

Another strong disengagement cue is a "halt hand"; in such a case, your baby will extend his fingers and wrist while moving his hand toward you or an object as if he were a traffic officer saying, "Stop!" Or your baby may make tight fists, bend his arms at the elbow, then raise the fists up and bring them suddenly down. This is a very potent cluster of cues. Similarly, but less dramatically, he may pound on his high-chair tray or table with the palms of his hands. Of course this will often happen when your baby is excited, and so don't automatically think of it as a negative cue; it may mean your baby needs a short break in the middle of his excitement.

Crawling or walking away from a person or object is another very common way that older babies show you they need a break, if for only a few seconds. A younger baby or a baby who has to stay in one place may just pull away or push away when he wants more space between himself and an object or person. The baby who shakes his head from side to side or completely turns away his head and eyes is saying the same thing. Finally, a sign that you may first notice in a newborn, but that may appear throughout the first year, is an arched back. By responding quickly to these signs of distress, you show a respect for your baby which will later translate into a positive sense of self. Ignoring them leads him to conclude, "You don't think I'm worth it, my signals aren't worth noticing."

Just as your baby signals, in subtle or strong ways, when he would like to disengage, he has many ways to tell you when he is ready to interact. A young baby's face may brighten when he wants to invite your attention. His eyes will widen, and his face will light up. He may open his hands slightly, one at a time. There may even be a flush in his cheeks and his eyes will sparkle. More subtly, when your baby first wants to interact, he may just lift his head and eyes toward you. Your young baby may also bring his arms in toward his stomach, hands in fists, and his palms toward his body. You may remember a similar description under disengagement cues, but this time your baby's hands will not move over his stomach as if they were lost or searching. You may see this new position toward the end of a feeding when the baby is in your arms. Not as hungry now, he is able to say, "I'm ready to be sociable as you feed me."

Strong engagement cues start with the eyes. Watch the way your baby looks at you. When you turn to face him and find that he has been looking at your face, he is ready to interact. When you are looking into each other's eyes, he is giving you a strong signal of readiness. Your baby may break off the gaze first—maybe only for a second and then he will be back again. Babies often repeat this pattern of looking and then looking away. Mothers are usually steady in their gaze and less likely to be the ones to look away first. Watch also the strong engagement cues of cooing and open, relaxed hands and shoulders. The feet may bike pedal then stop, as if waiting for your turn.

From a few weeks old to a year, babies tell us when they're receptive and when they need to think things through for themselves. Strong or subtle, their cues are the secret to successful exchanges.

The Basic Signals

As the months pass, your baby develops a much wider range of reactions to life experiences than "approach or avoid." The basic emotions of the first year are joy, interest, surprise, sadness, boredom, anger, disgust, fear, and pain. Each is associated with discrete signals. Through photographs of twenty-one babies and their parents, you will see these signals in action. You'll sharpen how you observe your baby's expression of emotion, in everything from tongue position to cheek muscles to the position of a shoulder. The photographs show that many signals are universal among babies, and they show that each baby has an individual style, too. Compare the photos to your baby when you're playing together, and you'll get to know your baby's vocabulary.

Although you'll best learn the signals by looking at the photos, here, for your quick reference, is a roundup of the cues of the basic emotions.

JOY. Eyebrows relaxed. Lower eyelid raised. Seen often are wrinkles in the outer corners of the eye and below the lid. Cheeks raised. Mouth may be parted. Lip corners can be drawn up and back.

INTEREST. Mouth and eyes relaxed. Eyebrows slightly raised. Upper or lower lip squared. Cheeks moderately raised.

SURPRISE. Eyebrows curved and high. Forehead wrinkled. Eyelids drawn apart. Jaw dropped. Mouth relaxed.

SADNESS. Eyebrows and upper eyelids' inner corners drawn up. Triangle formed under eyebrows. Lip corners down. Lips may be loose and trembling. Mouth open for crying. Chin tightening or wobbly.

BOREDOM. Eyes dull, don't appear to blink. Face sober. Mouth closed. Arms at sides. Baby immobile, looks drowsy.

ANGER. Brows strongly knit and lowered, often with a vertical line between them. Eyelids tense. Eyes have strong stare and may bulge. Lips pressed tightly together—corners are straight or down. Lips may be open and tense as if to shout.

FEAR. Eyebrows raised and knit. Forehead wrinkled. Upper eyelid is raised, lower is tense. White of eye visible under upper eyelid. Lips tense, drawn back, and open.

DISGUST. Eyebrows lowered, which in turn lowers upper eyelid. Eyes may narrow due to lowered upper eyelid. Nose wrinkled. Cheeks raised. Lower lip raised or protruding.

PAIN. Combines surprise with anger and irritability. Jaw dropped with mouth corners down. Eyes staring with eyelids tense. Cheeks raised as if questioning. (Not photographed for this book.)

How to "Talk" with Your Baby

At this point you may be wondering if you've missed some expressions and their meanings and have somehow fallen down on your parenting. You're a better "baby reader" than you know. And don't worry—your baby is always ready for you to "get it right." Even if he's whining, refusing to eat, and in general giving you a hard time, he's open to your approaches. He's saying, "Tell me you know what's going on inside me, then show me the way, and I'll change—just you wait and see."

Begin every observation of your baby with calm and quiet. Wait to see where he is heading. Gently mirror and echo his gestures. Try to breathe regularly and in sync with him. Use your peripheral vision to monitor the feet, hands, and shoulders as well as the face. Don't just watch his large eyes— notice his eyebrows, cheeks, and other face parts as well.

Eliminate interruptions by pets, phone calls, or other people. If the baby notices something, bring it closer or help him reach it. Say simply what you're doing before you do it to smooth over transitions. Try to move calmly and purposefully. Respect your baby's dignity by always making eye contact, pausing, and signaling that he's about to be picked up.

Bring an open mind to your observations—your baby will often surprise you. I'm reminded of a ten-month-old named Vinny who had developed quite a reputation. When put down on the floor to play after meals, he always rolled or crept under the bedroom dresser. On his side, facing the wall, he'd stay still for five minutes. His mother told me it was his way of turning his back on her and the household. When I came by, I got down on the floor to see what he was doing. There was an ant track, and our scientist was observing the insect world. He was clearly signaling keen interest, not hostility—his eyes were open wide, his lips were slightly parted, and his hands were relaxed.

Remember that all babies develop at their own pace. Age-linked developmental milestones are only approximations. Babies also form their own distinctive patterns of signals. Once you've learned the universal language of babies, you have to discover your baby's own style.

If your baby was born prematurely, you will have to be especially sensitive to his self-protective signals. It takes longer for preemies to calm themselves because their nervous systems can't handle strong stimulation. They may be more irritable and less organized, avert their gaze more often, and smile less often. Your preemie will be exquisitely aware of your emotional signals, so you have to be careful not to decrease his joy or make him angry. Also, protect him from well-intended relatives who may come on too strongly because they don't know his protective signals. Preemies do usually catch up to their full-term peers, although it may take as long as twelve months.

As you become increasingly attuned to your baby's messages, you will be giving pleasure not only to your baby, but also to yourself. There's no greater thrill than to hear and see your baby's growing personality. Just as infants love to be understood, parents love to understand.

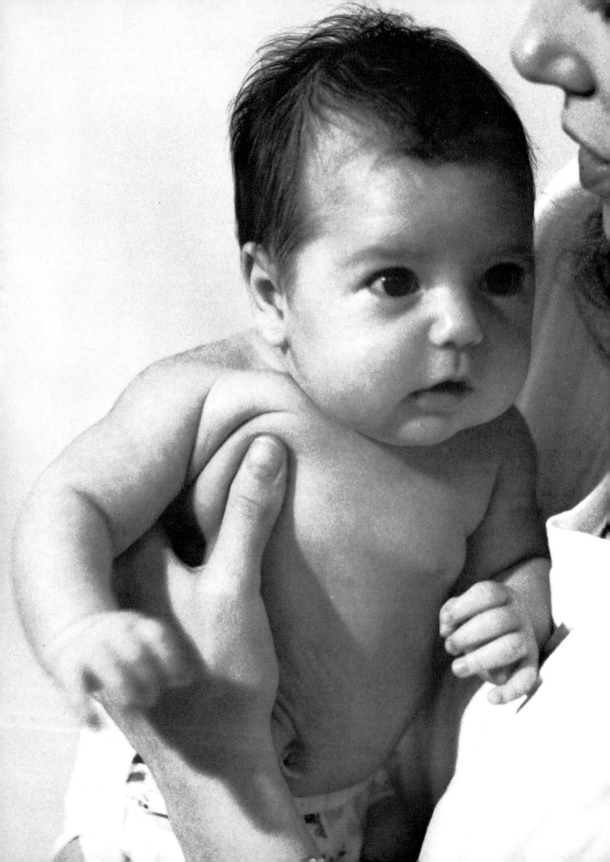

Birth to Three Months

A baby's earliest communications are crying, shutting down, staring, and being quietly alert. You want to help your baby achieve that last state as often as possible. A relaxed, alert baby is most receptive to new information. As you watch your baby in this mood, you'll see interest, distress, delight, loss of interest, and many other moods flicker into place, then take root or disappear. Quiet alertness can and should be established time and again.

Whatever you're doing when the baby is quietly delighted, continue it. Don't choose that time to brush hair, change the diaper, force a kiss. "Run the clock" as long as possible. If you use the quiet, alert time to make phone calls or get some work done, you're missing your baby's best time. A smiling baby is telling you to continue what you're doing; so pay attention!

Sometimes your baby will be alert but not quiet and relaxed. She's in a state of strained alertness. Her eyes are focused on the object of her interest, but they look fixed and concentrated, as if they belonged to a student who was anxious during an exam. The baby's facial muscles are tense and stiff. She's having trouble organizing her feelings. You can help her by being quietly supportive. If you try to open an exchange now, you'll disorganize her further and soon see tears.

Another indication of an infant in difficulty is a passive expression with slack facial muscles. When a baby's face looks that way, usually it's because she wants to tune out. Glazed eyes express the desire to "lower the volume" in the room—be it sound, light or activity.

A third indication of a disorganized infant is rapid changes of expression. A baby whose look quickly goes from strained to glassy to averting to unfocused and floating is quite likely experiencing distress. Before you respond, wait to see what state the baby ends up in. Then soothe her with a gentle, quiet rocking movement from side to side.

In the early months, the approach/avoid signals described in the opening section are especially important. They help you regulate your baby's mood so she's neither overly excited and distressed nor understimulated and bored. For example, if your baby's eyes are glazed and her head is slumped, she's trying to tune out. If her eyes are alert, then she's organizing herself. If you position her head so she can see better, you may help her maintain the alert gaze.

Your baby may turn her head in a relaxed manner during most interactions, but if the turn is sudden and approaches ninety degrees and stays there, she's upset and is trying to calm herself. It may be a few minutes before she turns her full face back to you. Wait until she decides. Your baby learns how to cue you to stop and start interacting so she can remain comfortable.

Crying is, of course, the most obvious disengagement signal. It's important to know that the faster you respond to crying, the less crying and the more periods of quiet alertness you'll have. The more predictably you cuddle, rock, feed, or give the pacifier, the better the nursing, the more eye contact, the faster the burp. Some brief crying can even help a baby soothe herself.

If you listen carefully, you'll soon learn to distinguish your baby's different kinds of cries. The pattern of a basic or hunger cry is an initial cry followed by a brief rest, a short breath in, a rising and falling melody, another brief rest, then a cry. The angry cry is turbulent and isn't melodic. The pain cry is a sudden, loud, long initial cry followed by a long rest. She'll breathe in, rest, then let go with a basic cry. The pleasure cry has a flat, nasal variable pitch. It is an early form of infant babble and is a way the baby entertains herself.

If you have an infant under three months, there may be some solace in knowing that crying and signaling in general become less intense as your baby learns that her needs will be met. She may even learn to wait a few minutes.

By noting the early warning signs, you'll be able to head off distress before it turns into crying. Look for brows drawn together and down, causing a crease and muscle bulge above the bridge of the nose. The mouth corners clearly pull down or sideways. The upper lip pulls up. The baby becomes restless, then fussy. She'll gaze down or narrow her eyes.

There are positive signs when a smile is on the way, too. Look for brows slightly drawn together but not lowered, wide eyes, a long look at you, pursed or protruding lips, a relaxed lower face, and partly sagging cheeks. The face is still, and the arms and legs are quiet. Pleasure is on the way.

If you're playing with your young baby and she laughs, it may be wise to stop further stimulation and wait. You have to watch closely to see when your baby wants to stop a simple game. Certain cues while she's laughing are attempts to keep out more stimulations. Laughing infants narrow or close their eyes and move their heads back. If you keep pushing, your baby may turn away her eyes, become distressed, and cry.

By watching your young infant's cues, you will get to know what sustains her attention. To stimulate your baby, try showing her objects that have high contrast or move in an interesting way. Keep it simple, because young infants easily lose interest when they're confused.

During these first months, as you imitate your baby and she mimics you, she is learning to amplify weak cues and moderate her emotions.

"Let's talk."

Over the next minute, Lauren and her mother will enjoy a quiet exchange. Here her mother picks her up and notices that Lauren wants to open an interaction. The one-month-old is quiet and alert, and she's making direct eye contact. The corners of her mouth are drawn up and back, as if she's getting ready to smile.

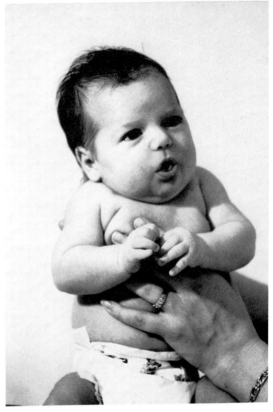

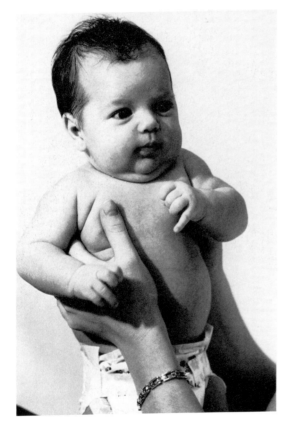

Seconds later, Lauren is saying that she's really interested in her mother's quiet voice. Her lower lip and tongue are totally relaxed and receptive. Another clear sign is that her hands are slightly raised, and she's holding her loosely fisted hands upward. Newborns learn best in a relaxed but alert state like this one.

Lauren has been pleased by the exchange. Even though most parents think their babies don't smile until six to eight weeks, even newborns show their pleasure by a general brightening. The signs are subtle. Lauren's eyes are brighter, and the corners of her mouth are up. Her right hand is reaching out a bit, another sign that she's receptive. This is the time a baby is most open to eye-blink games and mutual imitation.

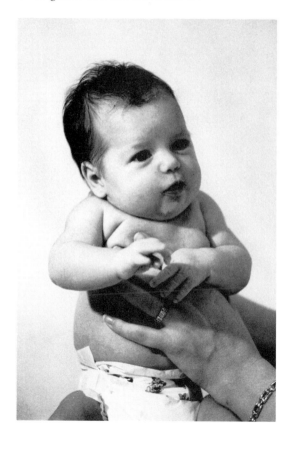

Lauren has broken off the exchange so she can digest it. Her head tilts back, her eyes are gently shut, and her eyebrows, cheeks, and lips are relaxed. Babies—and adults, too— have this sort of expression when they're savoring and remembering a good thing. This mood should not be interrupted, as her happy memory is forming.

"You got my attention."

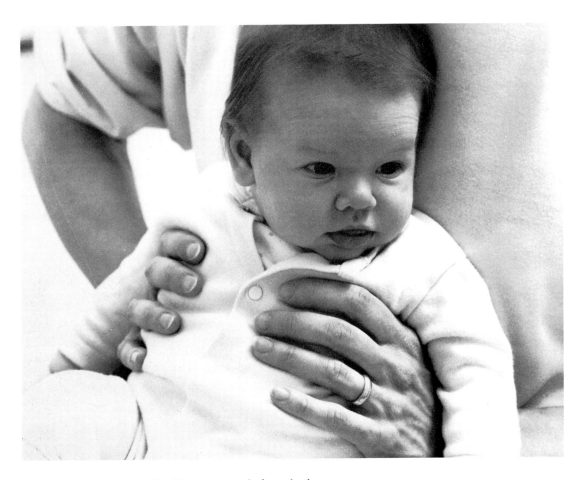

Here's Kayla, a seven-week-old, a moment before she becomes
alert and open to an exchange. Her eyes are dull, her cheeks
sag, her tongue dangles in her mouth, and her arms hang
limply at her sides. She's not involved or focused.

After her attention has been captured, her eyes brighten, her cheeks and upper lip become tight, her head raises off her chest, and her tongue is pulled back. Now Kayla is ready to talk.

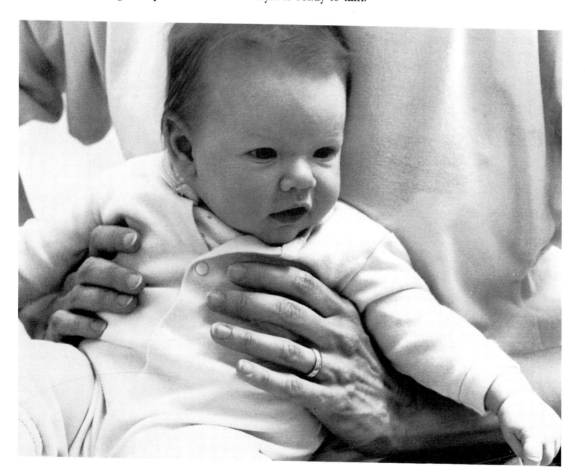

"I'm pleased."

A newborn's pleasure ebbs and flows. Within seconds, Kayla moves toward and then away from pleasure. First her whole face is lit up. The mouth is open, its corners turned up. Her tongue playfully feels her upper palate. Her cheeks are raised, causing telltale wrinkles under her eyes and alongside her nose. She'd like her mother to continue doing what she's doing.

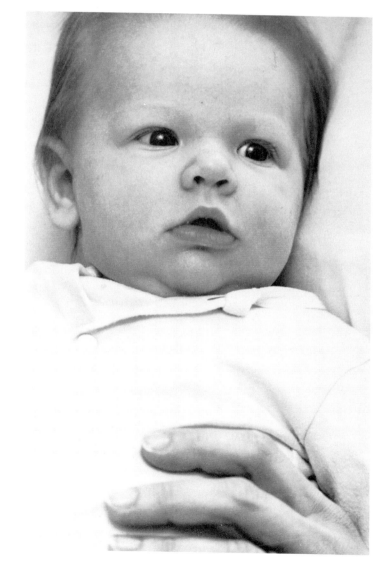

As she withdraws, her lower lip pulls down, and the upper one looks like a tent. The wrinkles are gone. This signals her mother to become quiet, to stop what she's doing. Then her mother can shift back to what Kayla was enjoying.

This is one of those first
smiles that all new parents
live for. There's no mistaking
the message in these bright
eyes. Dimples like these happen when the cheeks are
raised high in pleasure.
A smile like this one, which
bares the gums and brings
the mouth corners up, shows
not only pleasure but recep-
tiveness. Like our adult social
smile, the longer it lasts,
the better.

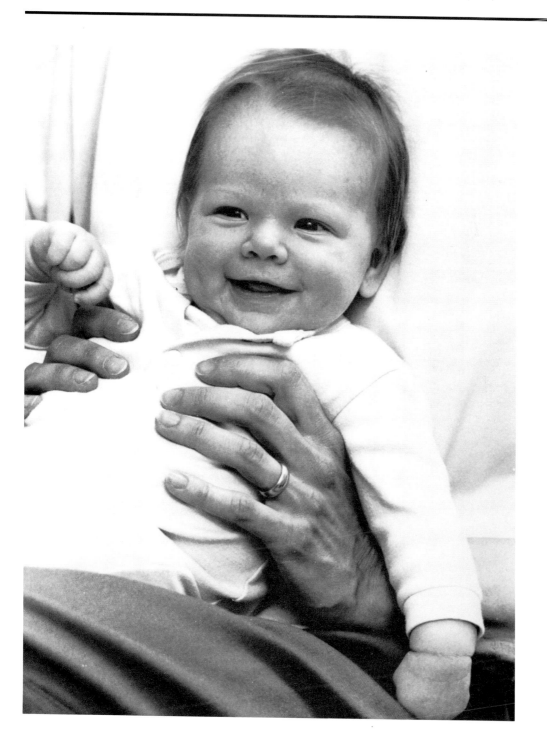

"I'm puzzled."

This two-month-old's knit brows show that he is very puzzled. Christopher sees something over his mother's shoulder that confuses him. His jaws have dropped in surprise, and his eyebrows are questioning. His attention has been caught, but he's not in the quiet, alert state conducive to learning. On the edge of distress, he'll need to be calmed before he's ready to take in what has happened.

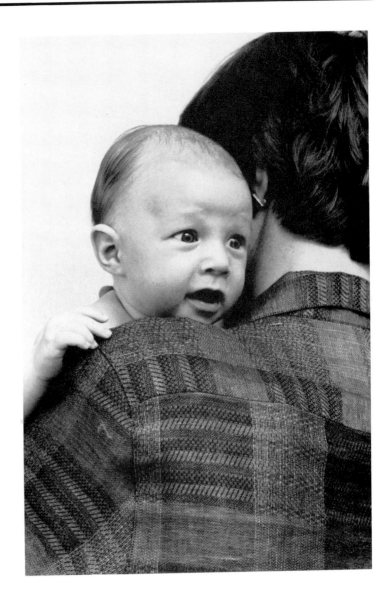

Kayla's cheeks, which were so high when she was happy, now droop. Her extremely knit brow and protruding lower lip show that she's upset as well as puzzled. She's keeping her head from turning more fully toward the event as a self-protective gesture. She shouldn't be turned or brought closer to what she doesn't like.

"I'm afraid."

Lauren is saying she's afraid to be held up in a sitting position. Her eyes are open so wide that the white shows above the iris. Her head is staying sunken into her shoulders, and her vigilance could easily slip into distress.

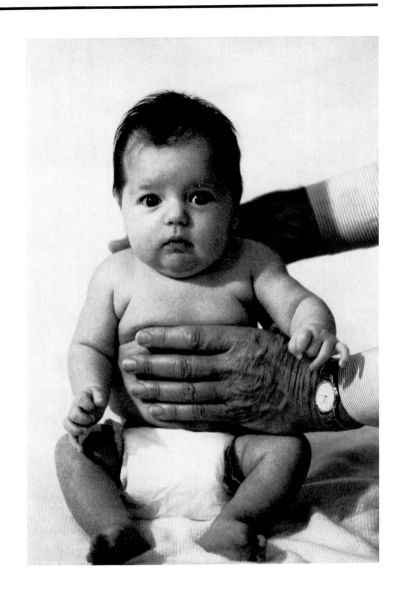

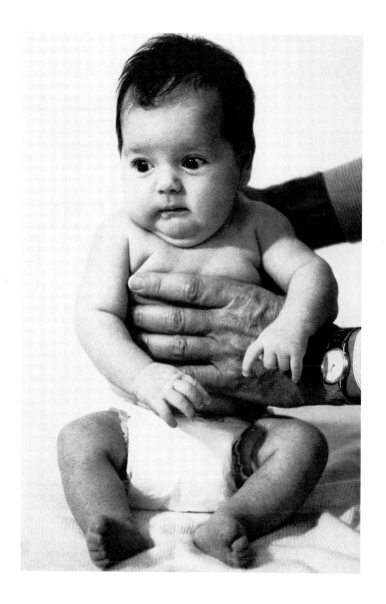

Then she turns and lowers her head, which are indirect cues to break off what's happening to her. Her arms move across her stomach as if to protect herself. Her tense mouth shows her fear, too; she's pulled in her lower lip and has clenched her jaw. Clearly she doesn't like this unfamiliar position.

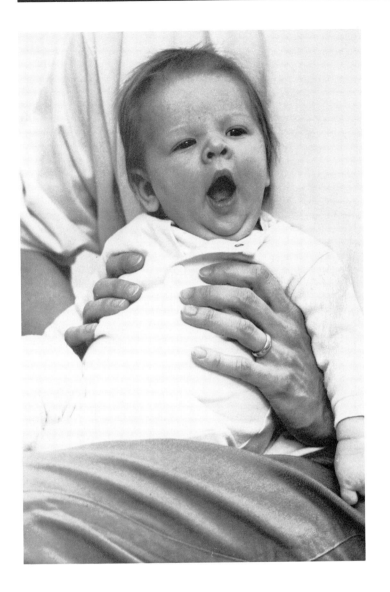

Most parents assume that a yawn means their newborn is sleepy. But it is not that straightforward. A yawn means the baby has had too much stimulation and wants to shift to a more relaxed level—perhaps through sleep but not always. Other signs can send similar messages: snoring, sneezing, hiccuping, increased sucking noises, and whimpering. Kayla yawns to pause for a second. Her eyes remain bright and focused on the action, and her shoulders are relaxed. Her head is up.

Christopher very much wants to break off contact. His head is on his chest, and his shoulders are shrugging. The tightly closed eyes and low brows are strong signals that he's had too much. He's shouting his yawn.

"I'm really scared."

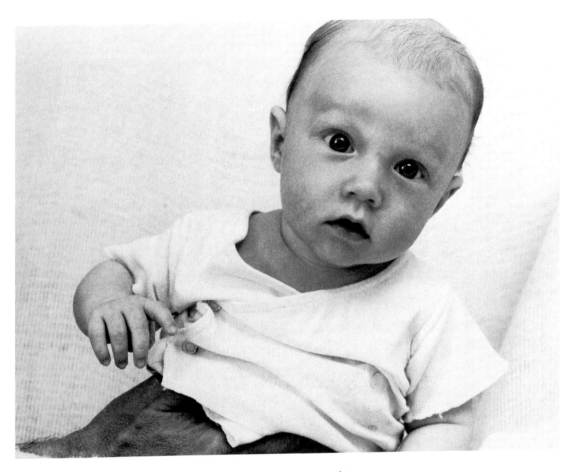

Poor Christopher gets increasingly uneasy as he's held upright. At first, he's rather surprised by this new perspective on the world, so his jaw drops and his eyebrows go up. When he's older and wants to stay "stop," he may put out his hand like a police-man; for now, he spreads his fingers to say the same thing.

Then he looks away from his father, a strong disengagement
signal. Other cues are his tight fist, arms slightly raised away
from trunk, shrugged shoulders, and head tensely held by
his neck muscles. Fear is shown by the whites of his eyes above
the iris.

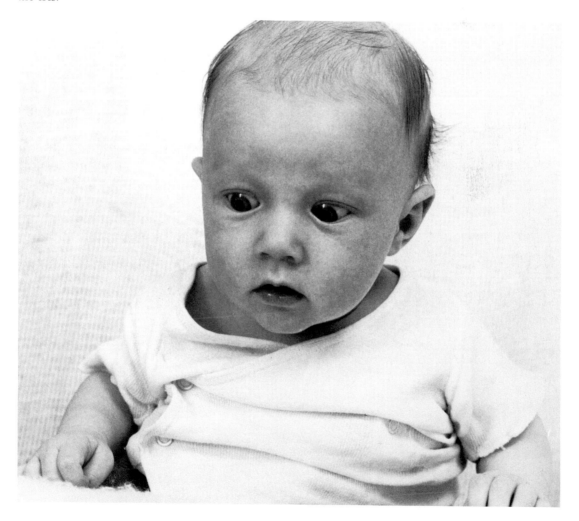

"Be more gentle with me."

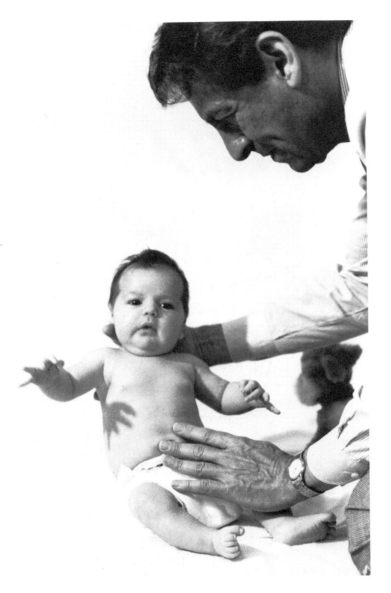

In the first month, a fear of falling calls out the dramatic Moro Reflex. Arms and legs fling out, and fingers and toes spread widely. Amy even hyperextends her little finger. The back often arches, too. The Moro Reflex is a call for more gentleness and quiet. Sudden changes of position or temperature or loud noises can lead to this startled response.

"Stop!"

Lauren doesn't like the approaching toy and face. Her tongue and hand are in stop positions. Her face is startled, and her head is tilting backward to get away.

"I've got to get away."

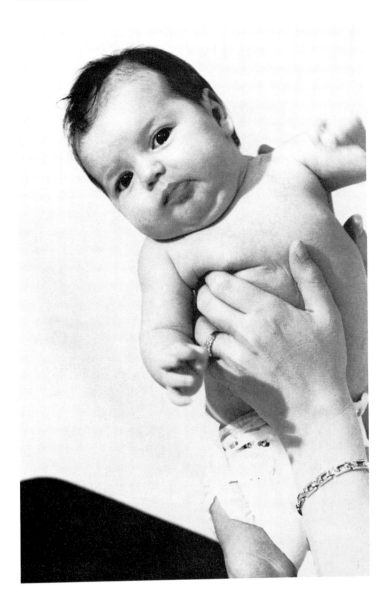

Lauren shows she wants out of the situation by arching her back. Here she's only mildly distressed and arches to one side to increase the distance from her mother. But she keeps eye contact—in fact, she's making an effort to hold her head up so she can keep her eyes fixed on her mother. Her lips are closed unevenly because her jaw is clenched.

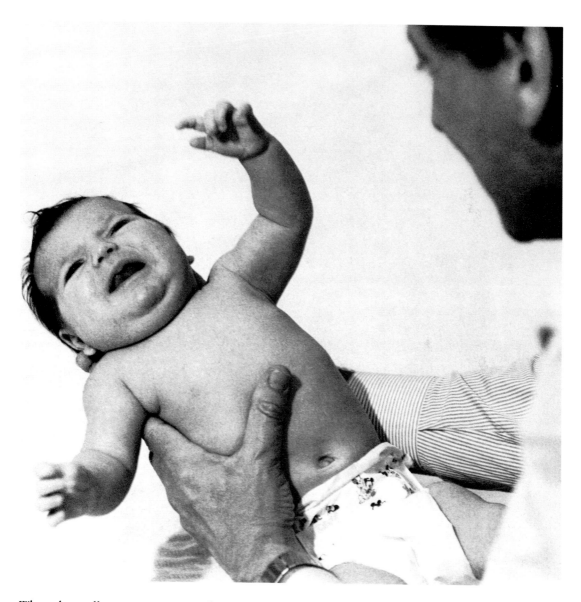

When she really wants to get away from me, she throws her
head back and looks up and away. Her eyelids are narrowing
and shutting down. She's also beating her arms overhead.
These are direct signs that a baby wants to suspend interaction.

"Cut it out."

Another expression that means "stop it" is the one adults
show when they say "ugh!" The pucker with raised upper lip
is the key. Lauren's nose is all wrinkled up as if she's just
smelled something unpleasant. Her brows are lowered into
a frown, another cue she wants to close the exchange. Her eyes
remain fixed on the unwelcome event as her head and shoulders
begin to turn toward the comfort of her mommy.

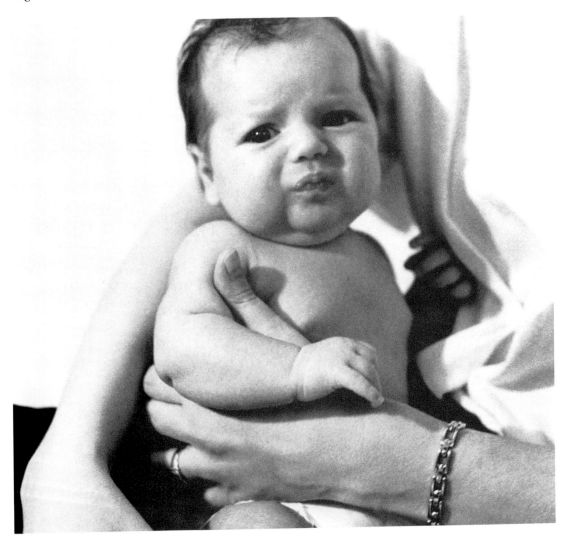

"Stop it."

Kayla wants to say "stop!" While keeping her eyes on her mother, she gives out strong signals that she'd like the situation to change: she sticks out her tongue quite far, clenches her fingers, wrinkles her brow, and turns her head.

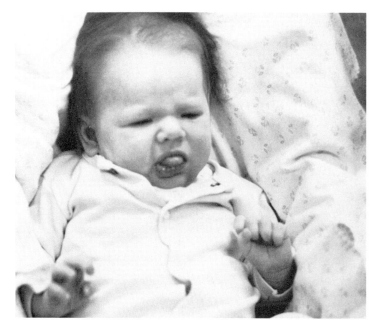

When that doesn't work, she shuts her eyes tightly, raises her wrists, and arches her back. Her tongue is eloquent even before she starts to use it for speech.

41

"Wah!"

Crying is an obvious signal that your baby is unhappy. While trying to shut out the world, his distressed cries are rhythmic, like hunger cries but more forceful. The bridge of the nose is deeply wrinkled as the eyebrows draw together, and tension of the cheeks causes deep lines. As you learn to spot your baby's subtler signals, you'll be able to respond before he has to resort to the extremity of crying. It is a great comfort to know when you can influence the direction of your baby's moods. Parents feel less in control once their babies cry.

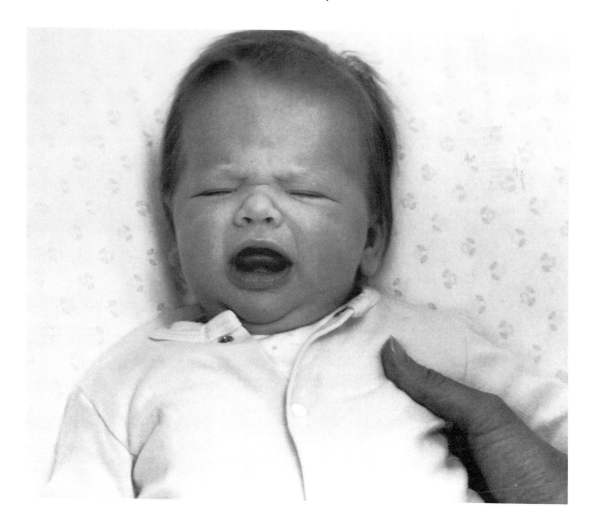

"I'm okay now."

Very rapidly, an unhappy baby can become a happy one, especially if you are in tune with her moods. Lauren is crying, sticking out her tongue, drawing in her brow, narrowing her eyes—all strong disengagement signals.

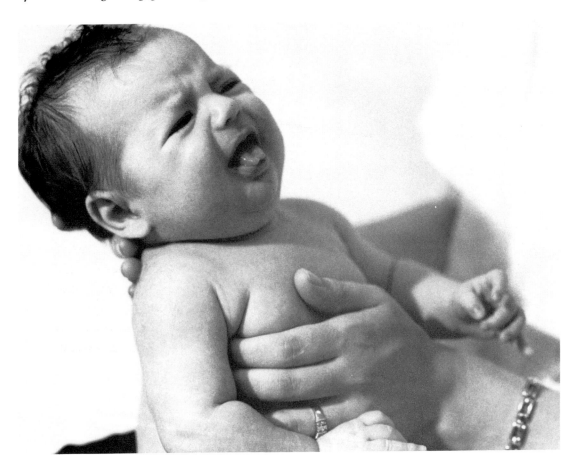

As Lauren's mother calms her down by talking quietly to her, Lauren's face becomes alert. Her hands find each other to comfort herself. Her lips relax, and her eyes focus on her mother's face. This clearly is helping her to gain self-control.

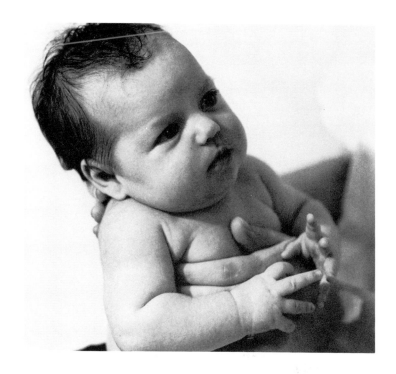

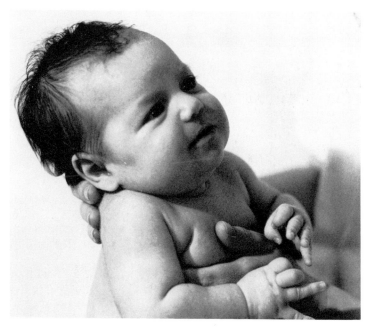

She's feeling very good now. Her eyes are bright, brows relaxed, and hands receptive. Now she's calm, alert, and ready to talk. This is a good time to start a face game or a song. If you respond quickly to your baby's cries, she will cry less and be in the quiet, alert state more often.

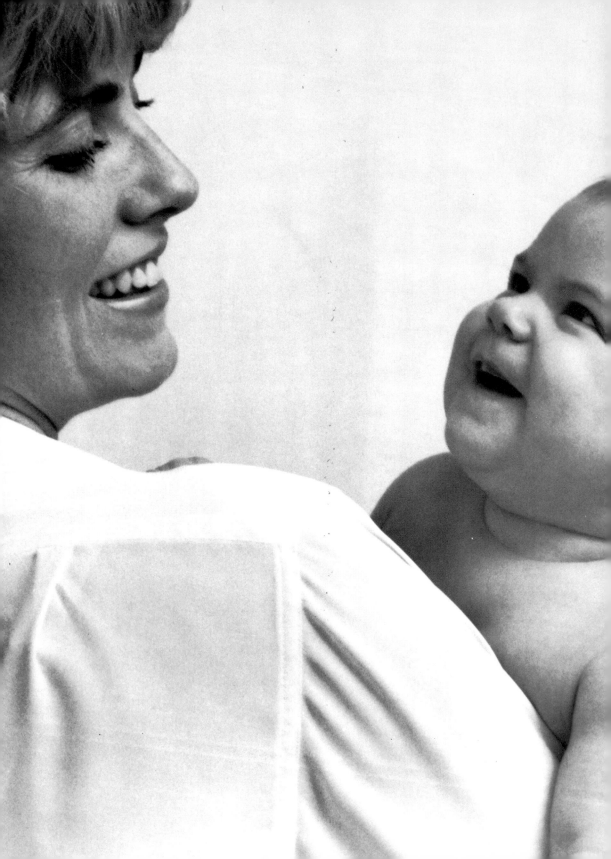

Four to Six Months

Toward the middle of the first year, your baby has many more ways to react to his experiences. He feels anger, surprise, sadness, fear, and joy. He's able to sustain his attention longer; instead of shutting down from too much stimulation, he's learned to step back for a moment—for example, by furrowing his brow slightly. Earlier he could only ignore something distressing or cry; now he can just study it until he figures it out. He's also learned to comfort himself, by playing with toys as well as his hands and feet, and putting them all in his mouth.

By four months, an infant's cues are clearly organized so you can take turns communicating. Let your baby know when it's his turn. Through moving your head and hands, dropping the pitch of your voice, becoming quiet, or moving your body away, you can cause your baby to smile, make sounds, or otherwise anticipate a lull. Toys can now help you build your relationship. "What are you looking at?" "Here, put this in your mouth instead." "Here's your bottle."

You can help keep your baby's attention by modestly exaggerating your expressions or varying the way you present an object. Such playful exchanges may cause your baby to prefer a particular adult, sibling, or object. He will signal this through prolonged expressions of interest and quiet alertness to them.

Your baby can be playful now, too. A four-month-old's smile can melt the most distracted adult. Peek-a-boo games engage siblings and strangers alike. They start with eye-blink games and a cloth hiding baby's face then being pulled away.

After about four months, infants can copy the sounds and faces of familiar people. They also remember behavior and imitate it later. Try sticking out your tongue or swiveling your head from side to side.

Your baby's cues are starting to take on larger meanings. Between three and four months, a smile can indicate not just happiness but also a desire to continue an action. It can also show a decrease in tension after a puzzlement is solved. Similarly, grimaces and frowns can show not only unhappiness but also a desire to change the direction of the action.

After three or four months, babies may be irritable or sad when they can't cause something to happen. Watch the misery on a five-month-old's face when (for 20 to 30 seconds) you keep your face still while he's trying to make you react.

During these months, there is a dramatic drop in crying and an increase in smiling. This happens because you've responded to crying quickly and effectively and have shown your own pleasure in mutual smiling. But sometimes infants whine as a halfway move. They're trying to signal discomfort in a less extreme way. Be grateful for this whine—it's more conversational than a cry.

Although you continue to be the greatest influence on your baby's developing emotions, by six months he will be looking at you less often. His interest is shifting toward toys, objects, and the rest of the world. To capture his attention, your face has to be expressive and positive, and your reactions have to be associated with his growing discoveries.

Also, after four months it becomes harder to know what led to your infant's knit brow or smile. Looking at the broader situation will help you interpret the cues.

"The ball is nice."

Like younger babies, infants from four to six months are most receptive when they're quiet and alert. Two clues are focused, expectant eyes and firm facial muscles, especially the cheeks. A relaxed baby's face isn't slack, but open and interested. After Rachel touches the spongy ball, she shows her quiet pleasure with bright eyes, relaxed lips and tongue. A quietly alert baby is open to new experiences. Saying her name or yours will associate words with pleasures.

"I'm open."

These babies are showing
varying levels of receptivity
to new experiences. Michael's
eyes are alert, but they're
a bit preoccupied. Though
he's in a quiet, alert state,
he's relaxing after a previous
exchange. When your baby
is in an open state, wait for
his eyes to focus before
making an overture.

Now Michael is quietly
alert. His eyes are open
wide, and he almost seems
to be holding his breath
in anticipation of something
good. He's done his relaxing.
Now he's poised and ready.

Kevin is extremely receptive
to the dog. He's so eager
to explore it that he's leaning
forward and grasping
it with both his hands and
feet. His alertness shows
in his focused eyes, relaxed
brows, firm cheeks, and
smile.

"I'm interested in my reflection."

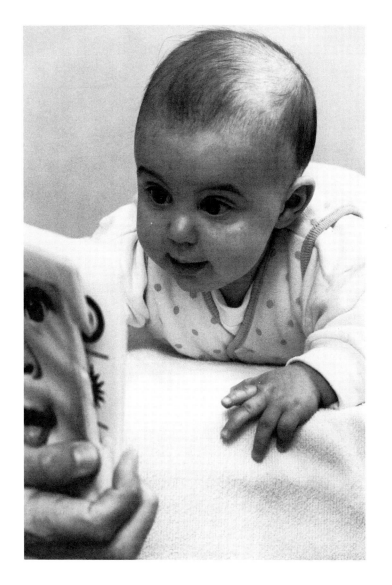

As Michael notices himself
in the mirror, his face
brightens. He goes from
a quietly open attitude
to pleasure. His lips are
first loose, then firm,
then smiling. His cheeks
become firm, and his
eyes open wider. His hand
fans out, possibly an early
form of pointing. His head is
raised by his neck muscles
to be in firmer control of the
happy spectacle. Positioning
an infant to be comfortable
when learning depends
on the individual infant's
preferences at the time.
By varying the position from
tummy to back to side,
you can expand learning,
too.

"I know you're looking at me."

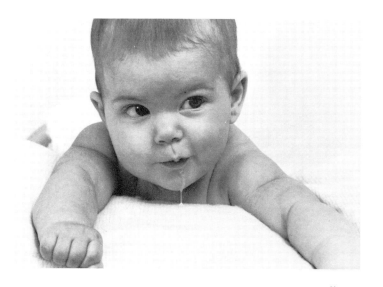

Jennifer is alert to her mother's attention, and she's playfully and charmingly showing it. First she twists her upper lip and turns her head in a different direction than her gaze. Then she tenses her upper lip during a puckered smile.

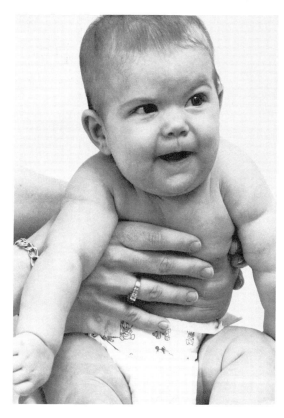

This happy grimace is to capture her mother's attention. She wants her mother to look where she's looking. Her brows are slightly knitted.

"I'm getting excited."

At first Kate is wary of the dog. She reaches out tentatively to explore it. Her face is open, but her neck muscles are tight and are holding her head alert.

She is surprised, encouraged, and pleased by what she finds. Her mouth and hand are open to take it all in.

When her mother pretends the dog is barking, Kate gets quite
excited and opens her mouth still wider in a broad smile.
Her hand is closed now, showing she's grasping the toy in her
imagination. This is an important sequence for Kate as she
was doubtful and then very positive. So long as she remains
interested, it would be helpful to repeat the game for as long
as possible.

"I'm uptight."

Rather than quiet and alert, Kevin is strained and wary. From
this tense position he could either end up withdrawn or pleased.
In strained alertness, the eyes are focused but look fixed.
Facial muscles, like Kevin's upper lip, are tight. Kevin is holding
his head back and is raising his eyebrows in curiosity.

Kevin has decided to be happy. He has a delighted smile.
His head and arms are moving forward. But his raised eyebrows
and shrugged shoulders continue to show he's tense. By putting
his hands together, he shows he's ready to reach out and hold
onto the stimulating toy.

"If you like the picture, I like it, too."

At first Sarah isn't interested in the picture. Her cheeks sag, her eyes are half closed. When she looks up and sees that her mother likes the picture, she gets interested. In the last photo, she's pleased, even though her mouth hasn't changed. The cues are subtler—sparkling eyes, firmer cheeks, a raised chin. Sarah's parents can help her use more obvious signals that others can easily read. Soon they can start playing face games and use exaggerated mouth gestures—which will be not only useful, but fun.

At first wary, Luis becomes happy after he explores the puppet.
Then he shuts his eyes to savor the experience, as if pushing
it into his memory. He wants to remember how nice and furry
the puppet was. If his parents pay attention to the last expression, they'll know it's their cue to let Luis quietly be until
he shows a shift of mood or interest.

"I'm content to be by myself."

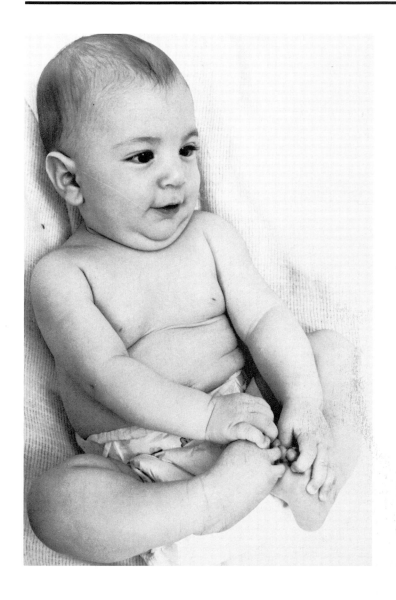

Joshua is quiet and alert, but he's self-absorbed. He's content to play with his feet. His whole body is relaxed, especially his shoulders. His eyes seem to be gazing inward. He shows his self-absorption by bringing his hands and feet together.

Now Joshua's coy smile is an invitation to open an exchange. Even his feet are opening up. It's helpful to note the difference between self-absorption and openness. If you offer a new toy or interaction while your baby is in an open mood, it is more likely to be appreciated.

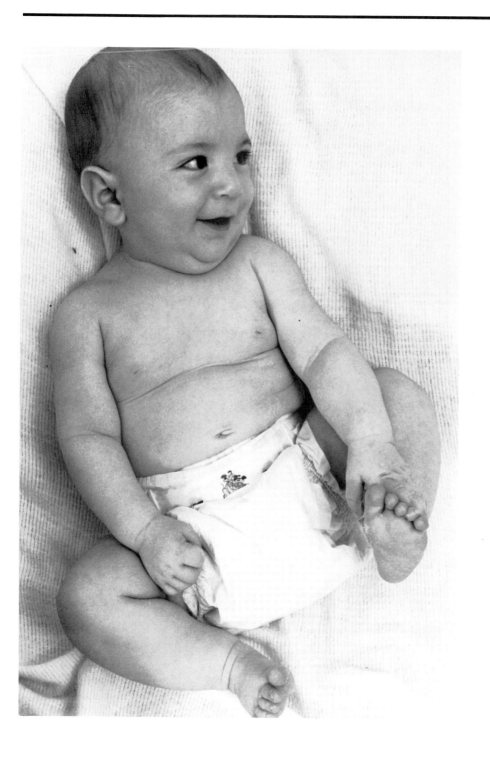

"I can stick my tongue out, too."

At five months, Joshua loves to mimic his parents—here, by playfully sticking out his tongue as his mother has. His bright eyes and smile show that he's enjoying the game. Sometimes, though, babies copy their parents without actually sharing the emotion behind the expression. They may mirror your smile with just their mouths but not their eyes, for example. So the mimicking that increases during these months should be enjoyed and watched closely as it expands and deepens.

"I'm curious about that.

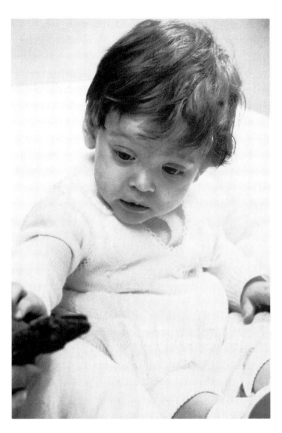

Relaxed lips and fixed gazes are classic signs of curiosity.
At five and six months, these babies are interested not only
in their immediate caregivers but in objects as well. These babies
want their parents to look at the toys, too, and comment on them.
It's important to respond to your baby's curiosity because
it shows him that the world corroborates his interests. Curiosity
is one of the easiest signs to respond to—except, sometimes
the baby's attention is fixed on something across the room,
rather than right in front of his face! This activity needs only
your quiet presence. When your infant is exploring, it isn't
necessary to add exclamations, names, or questions.

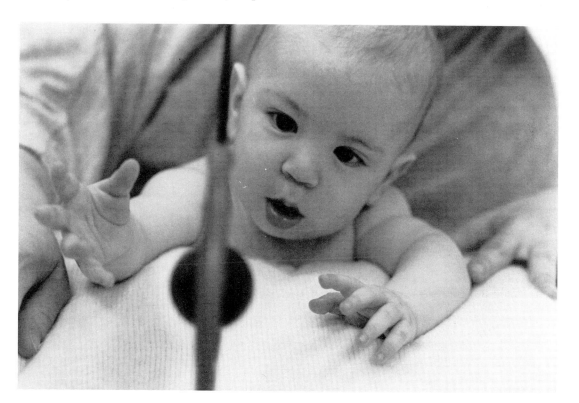

"Be gentle with me."

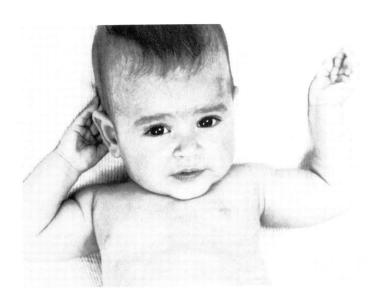

Some babies are easily startled by loud sounds, quick motions, and sudden appearances, so their parents have to be especially gentle when calling forth their curiosity. Six-month-old Emily, who was recently adopted, is learning to trust her parents and to calm herself. At first she is curious and stares intently at the object. But her knit brow and the hand on the ear shows she's already uneasy.

Then she is startled and becomes frightened, drops her jaw, cries out, and buries her head in her shoulder. As her mother waits calmly, Emily's arms, shoulders, and hands gradually relax and open as she calms herself.

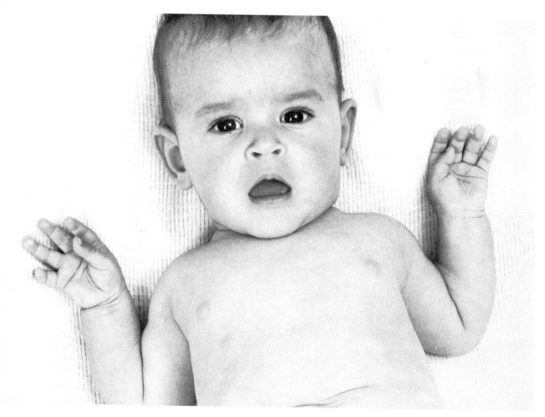

"Boy, am I uninterested."

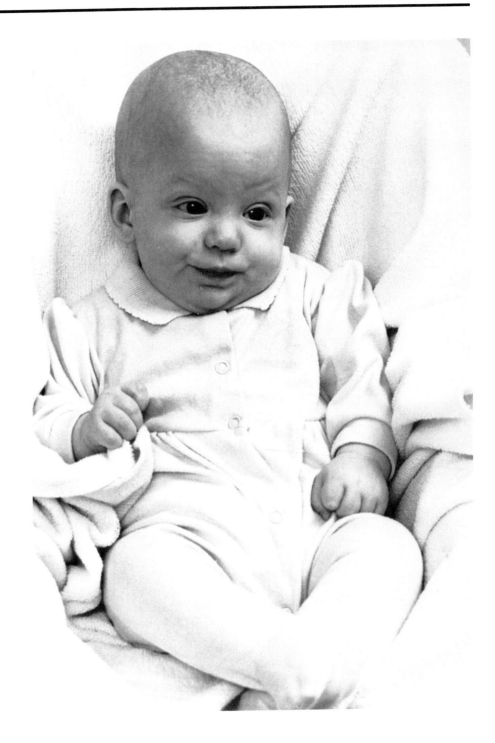

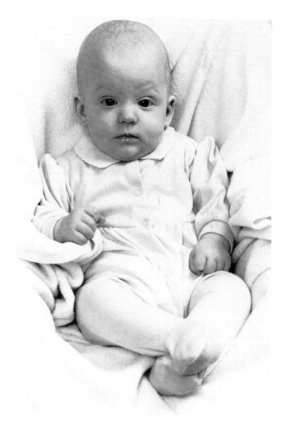

A moment of mild interest flutters over the face of this baby. Rachel's closed hands show she's not involved in the view from her seat. Then she grimaces to amuse herself, after which she has an even flatter expression. Rachel is an even-tempered baby with subtle signals, so her parents have to pay especially close attention to her cues.

"That looks great."

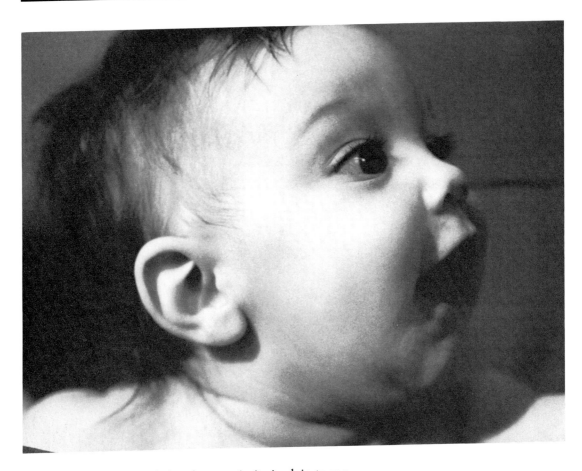

Kate is a very expressive baby whose curiosity is plain to see.
She's intensely interested in the new toy and expects to like
it. Her face is bright—head forward, chin up, mouth open, eyes
open, brows up.

Uh oh, she's disappointed, so she brings her head down, wrinkles her nose, brings her brows together and down, and clenches her fist.

"I'm puzzled! What's going on?"

These babies are curious and uneasy. They're intrigued yet confused. Curiosity is shown by their fixed gazes, relaxed mouths, and open hands. But their brows are knit, and one of the babies clutches his mother's sweater. A newborn, slightly distressed by a person or thing, turns away. These four- and five-month-olds can handle puzzlement and stay concentrated on the object of curiosity.

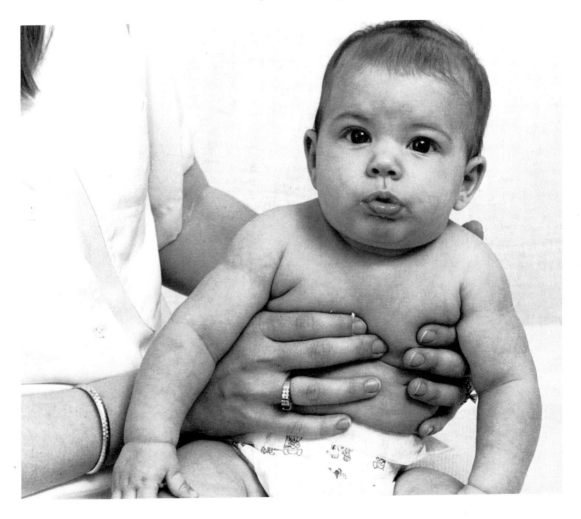

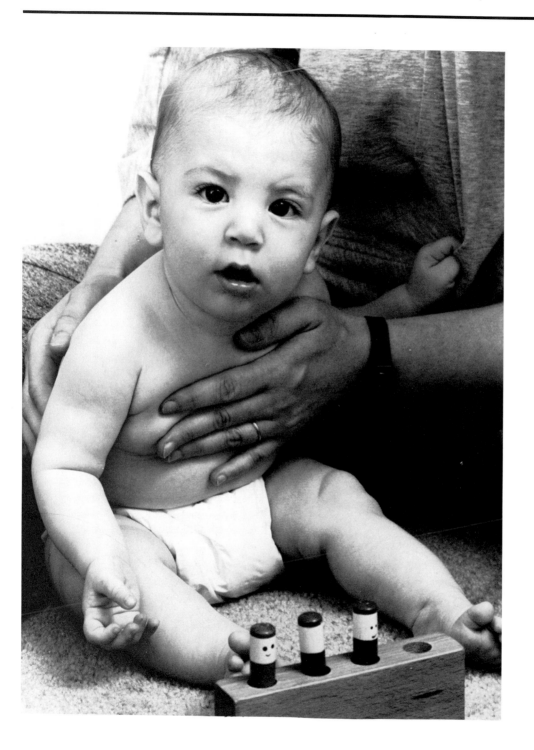

"I may not like that."

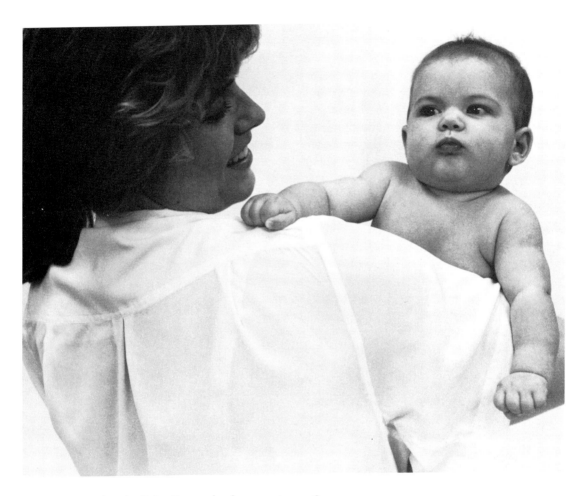

Curiosity mixed with slight distress leads to wariness. One
sign is a stiff body. As she looks over her mother's shoulder,
Jennifer stiffens her arms. She also clenches her jaw and
begins to turn her head away.

Rachel is stiff, too. Her shoulders are rigid. Her face looks sober. Although Jennifer's and Rachel's firm gazes show that they're interested in something, stress and nonreceptiveness are seen in their stiffness and tenseness. They're preparing to be afraid. This is the moment for a caregiver to provide a pleasing and familiar activity.

"I'm getting uneasy."

Kevin shows the blend of curiosity and fear known as wariness. Showing curiosity, his head is forward and attentive, and his mouth and hands are open and relaxed. But the wrinkled forehead, wide-open eyes, and lower-lip pucker show the beginnings of fear.

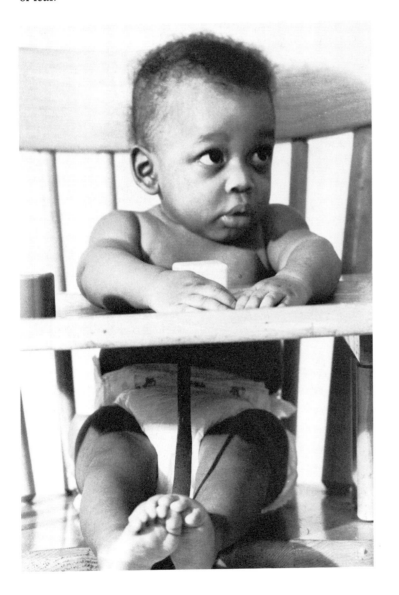

Michael is more afraid, and his clenched fists and wrinkled brow show it. The whites of his eyes and wrinkled brow show a baby who's expecting something unpleasant.

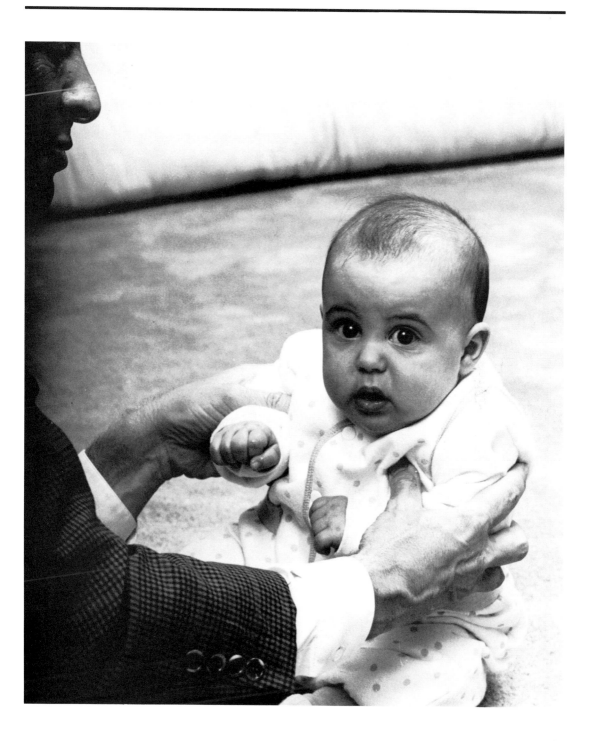

"Yikes."

Drew has just been startled—he looks like someone goosed him! His eyes are open so wide in fear that the whites show all around. His jaw has dropped in surprise. His brows are curved. He's startled, a mixture of fear and surprise, which is a cue to be more gentle. A whispered "what was that?" along with a hug can help an alarmed infant calm himself.

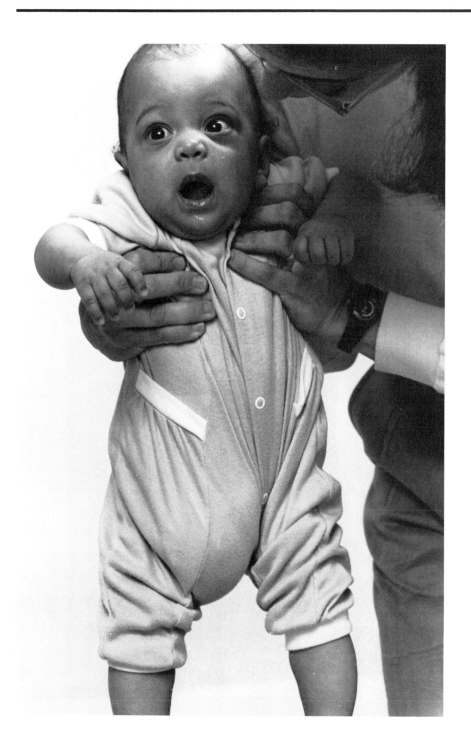

"The doggie is nice after all."

As Kate studies the dog, her wariness lessens. Here she opens
her eyes wide, tucks in her chin, and lifts her shoulder as
if to protect herself. She's guardedly optimistic.

When she decides the dog's okay, she stops being wary. The corners of her mouth turn up, her head lifts, and her shoulder lowers. A smile can indicate not only happiness but also release of tension, the end of doubt.

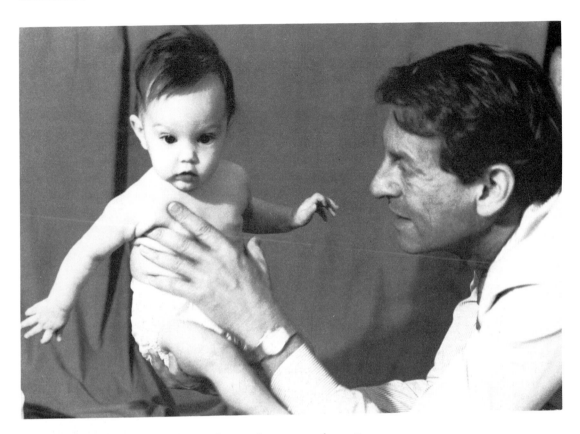

Kate's fear at being suspended in midair is shown most dramatically by her spread out, tense arms and fingers. Her eyes look hard. She's also surprised, which she shows with a dropped jaw and loosened cheeks.

When distracted with a funny face, she shows relief all over
her bright, smiling face. Her hands and arms are starting
to relax, too. Kate shows her restored good spirits with a happy
expression.

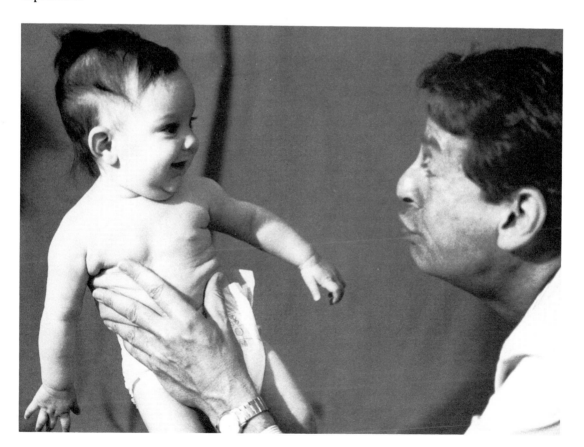

"That's too close."

When parents see that their babies are interested in a toy,
they often bring it closer. After the first months, many babies
prefer that interesting objects be no closer than a few feet
from their faces until reached out for. These six-month-olds
are telling their parents that they have come too close. When
Sarah's mother thrusts a toy close to her face, the baby closes
her eyes and turns her head away. Her lips tense, brows furrow.

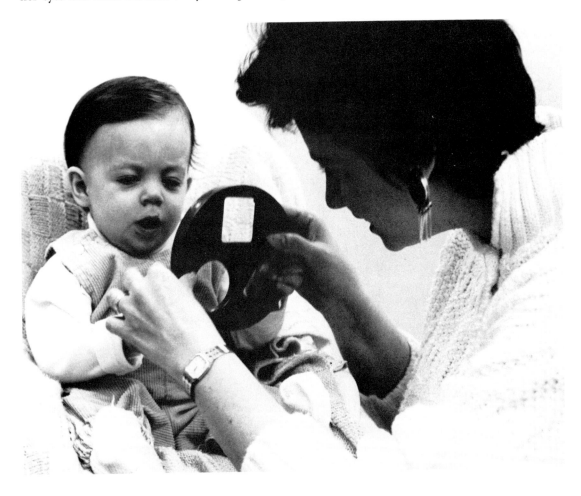

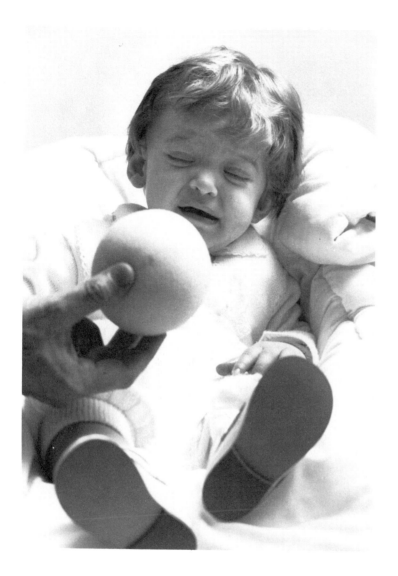

Brian is shutting down
completely because the toy
is too close. His lips and
cheeks are so tight that he's
grimacing, and his eyes
are strongly closed.

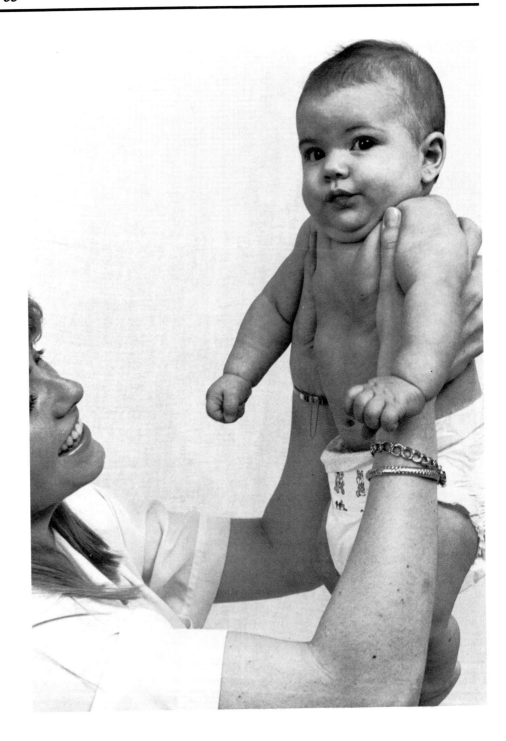

Sometimes when we're trying to amuse our babies, they tell us we're going too far. When Jennifer is held playfully overhead, she pointedly turns her head away from her mother. Her left hand posture says "stop," while the right hand clenches. Other signs that she's had enough are the puckered face, stiff elbow, and low chin.

Luis pushes his tongue out to show his distress. He's making a tight fist, too, and his eyebrows are drawn in. When you see disengagement signals like these, become quiet and give the baby time to reorganize.

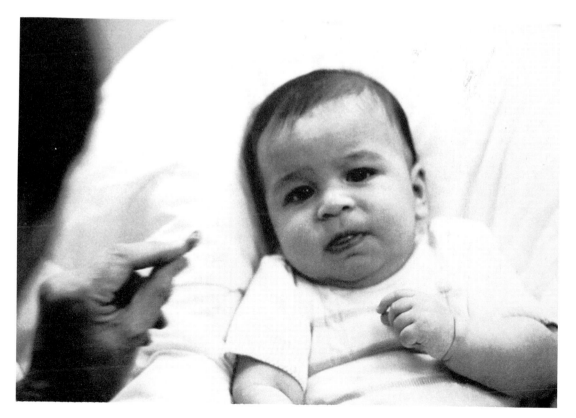

"Time out."

Often a tired appearance means that a baby has been pushed too hard, not that she's actually ready for a nap. Sarah needs some quiet time, and signals this by looking sleepy. Her brow is lowered, her cheeks sag, her eyes are dull and closing, and she's pouting. The stiffened finger may help her become more alert later on.

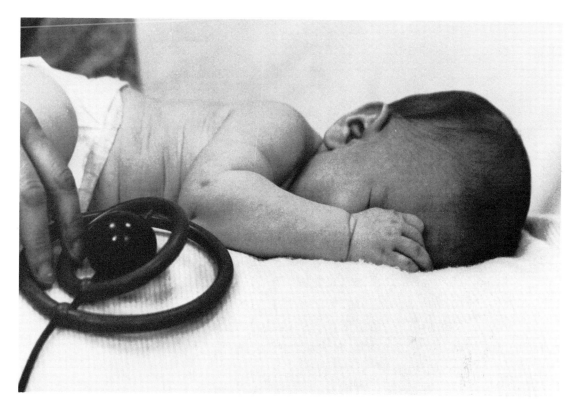

Joshua has really been pushed too far, so he's feigning sleep.
In this extreme example of shutting down, he buries his head
in a blanket and covers his face and tightly closed eyes with
his hand. Both babies are touching their faces to comfort
themselves.

"Stop moving and give me a chance to look at the rattle."

With some babies, it's easy to play too hard. Emily's mother is shaking the rattle to amuse her, but what the baby really wants is to study it quietly. At first she is puzzled. She lifts her head to satisfy her curiosity, but the furrowed brow shows she's uneasy.

The rattle keeps on shaking, so she pulls her hand and head back.

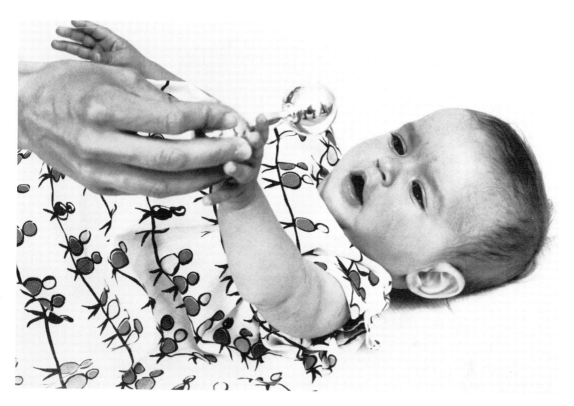

The rattle finally stops moving. She reaches for it as her face relaxes into a faint smile. It isn't clear whether her widespread fingers are saying "stop" or "let-me-hold-it."

A trembling lower lip says that crying is about to happen unless
you quickly comfort your baby. As Kevin sits in his high chair,
other signs that he's about to cry include his tightly flexed
feet and averted gaze. The corners of his mouth and cheeks
are sagging down.

Sarah is reaching to be picked up. Her forehead is deeply
creased and her eyes are slits. She has a grimacing expression
and tears are falling.

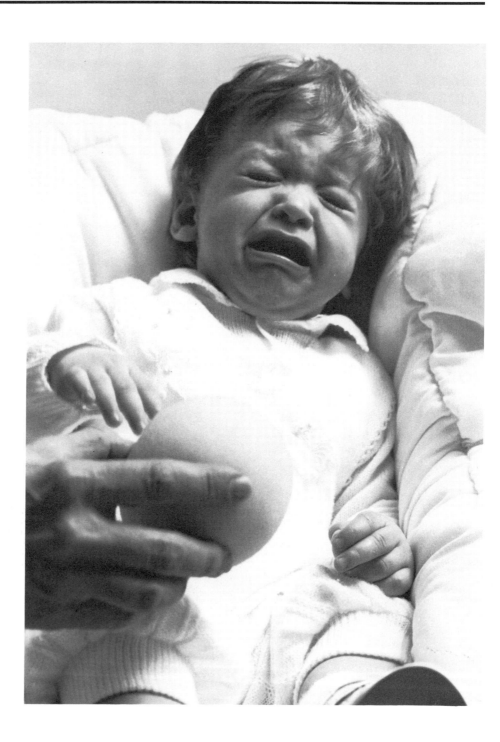

Crying is your baby's strongest signal of distress. But the body language is just a more intense version of the early warning signs. Both of these babies' eyes are closed tightly to shut out the unpleasantness, and their brows are furrowed as deeply as possible. The lower lip trembles and their toes and fingers fan out to say stop. As you become attuned to your baby's early signals, you'll have less crying.

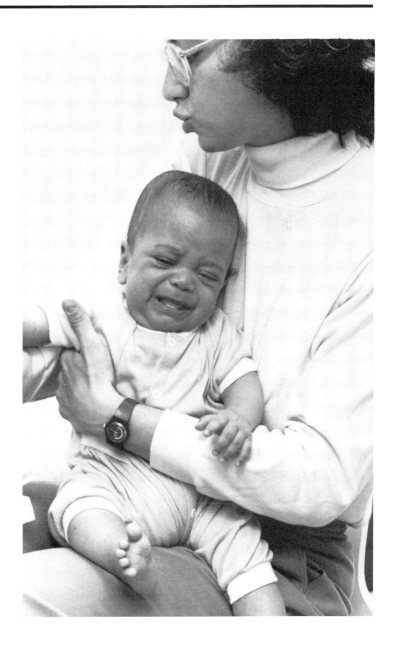

"I'm feeling a little better."

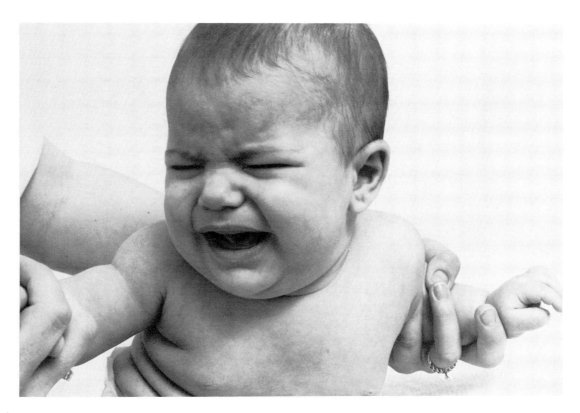

This whimpering cry is accompanied by a furrowed brow
and tightly shut eyes.

Then Jennifer starts to relax, first showing it in her cheeks and forehead. Her eyes are slowly opening. Her mother's attempts to comfort her are succeeding.

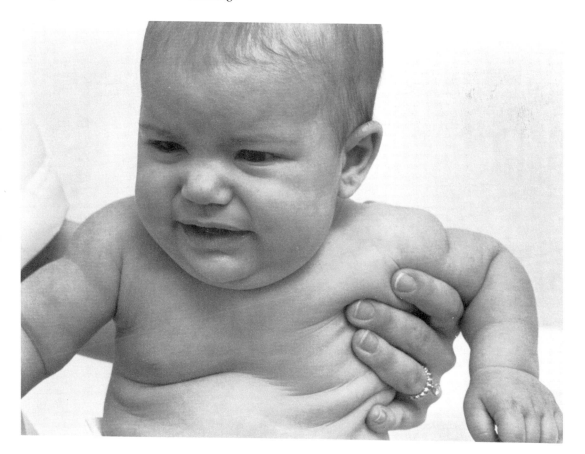

"I guess I'm okay after all."

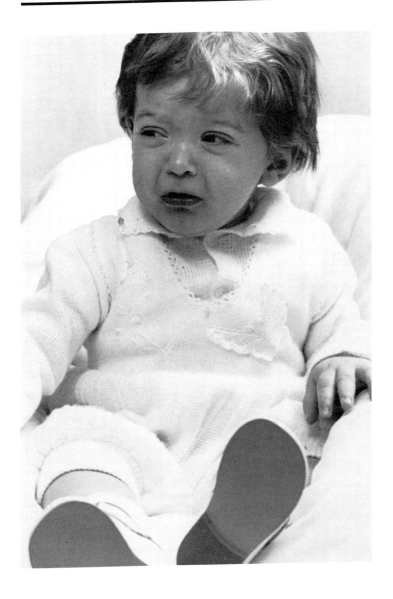

Brian is about to start crying. His lower lip quivers and his nose sniffles. His upper lip is very flat, his lower lip is trembling, and his eyes are narrow.

His mother distracts him with something pleasant. His bright eyes, smile, and raised head show that he has changed and is happy. The hand that was fanning out in distress has relaxed. Still, abrupt mood swings like this one show that a baby is feeling stress. It's time to slow down his experiences.

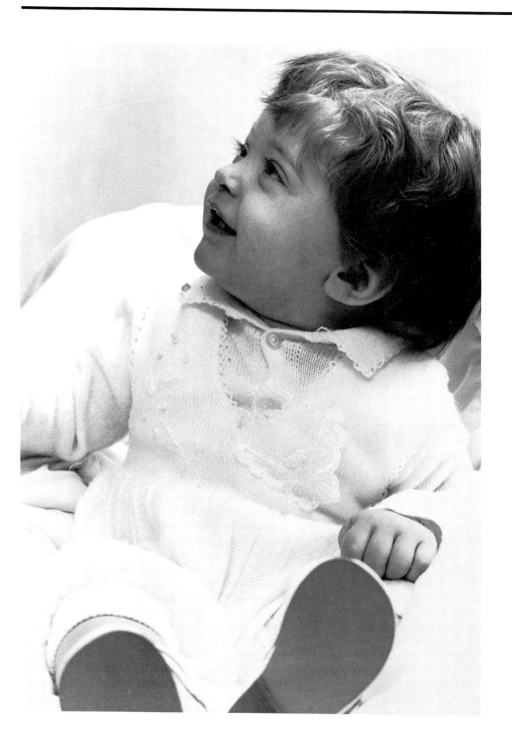

"I'm mad at you."

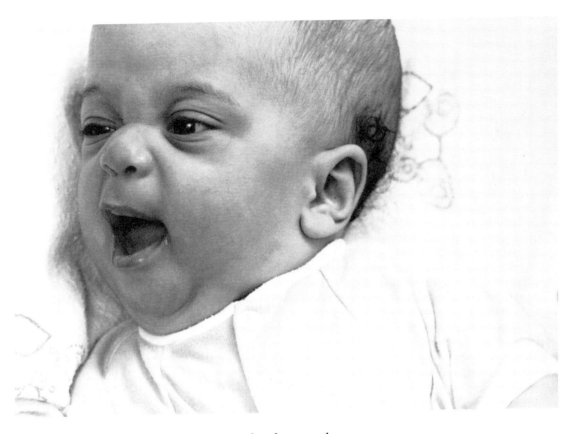

Younger babies can feel annoyed or irritated. A four-month-
old can begin to focus anger at someone or something. Drew
is trying to say something to his mother about his annoyances.
Here his eyes have a hard, bulging stare and his tense lips
form a square, shouting shape.

Then he pushes a tight fist at his mother, as if giving her the business. He averts his eyes and presses his lips firmly together.

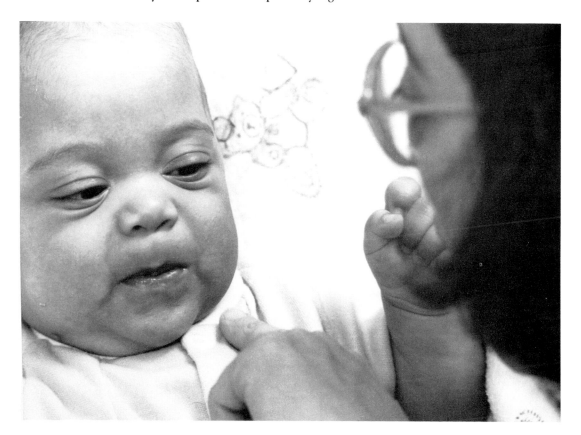

"I'm angry."

Anger can be subtle or very obvious. Emily shows her anger
in her hard stare and tight mouth. Cues she's distressed include
the hand on the back of her head, her furrowed brow, and
the tongue showing between her lips. Next time, her parents
will avoid what's provoked her.

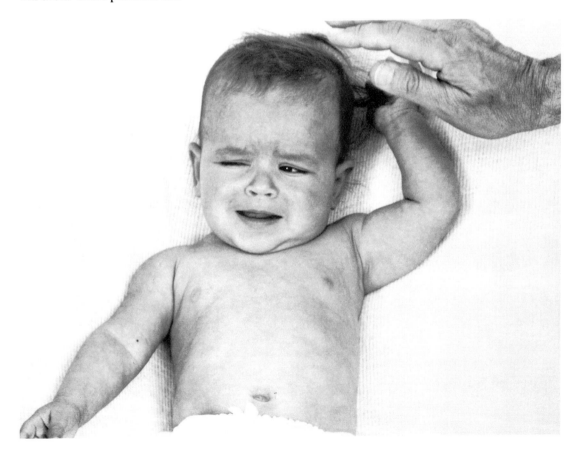

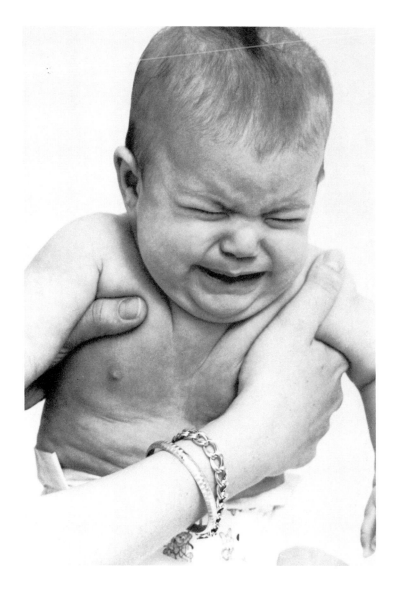

Jennifer has become enraged and is grimacing as much as she can. There are no tears and she is shouting.

"I'm disgusted."

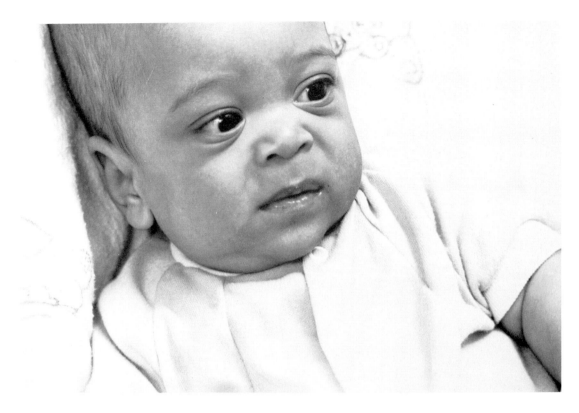

Also new during these months are expressions of disgust—
aimed perhaps at you, or perhaps at that first taste of cereal.
Drew shows mild disgust by wrinkling up his nose and raising
his upper lip in an adult-like expression. The raised brows
say that whatever has disgusted him took him by surprise.

Later, in a more extreme expression of disgust, he sticks out
his lips and tongue and averts his eyes. Moving his head down
and to the side says he wants the unpleasantness to stop. Again
the nose is emphatically scrunched up.

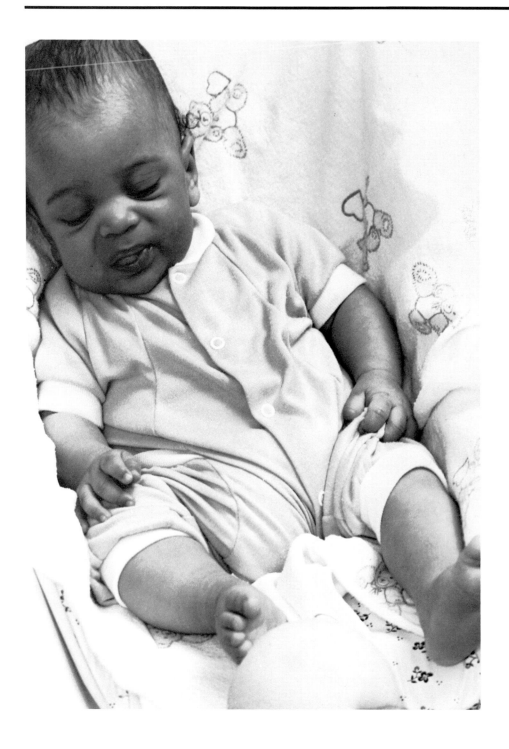

"That tastes horrible . . . but I'll live."

Expecting to like what's on the spoon, Kate is relaxed, receptive, and trusting.

But the bitter taste causes her whole face to grimace, wrinkle, and tense up. She is thoroughly disgusted by a taste of lemon juice.

She makes a quick recovery.
First to relax are her cheeks,
upper lip, and chin. She
intimates she could cry if
the bitterness persists.

Then her brows relax,
her lower lip drops open,
and her tongue sticks
out. She copes well with
disgust.

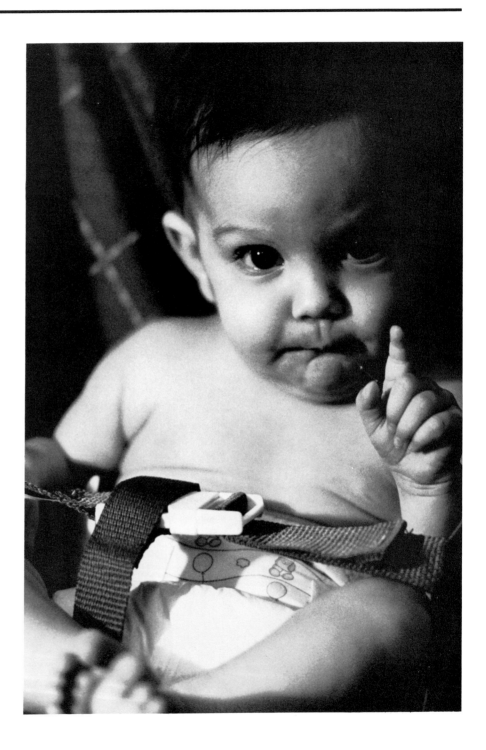

As your baby nears six months, you'll find she increasingly takes an active role in your interactions. Kate points her finger to direct her mother's attention. At five months, she's an early pointer. At first her brows are knit and questioning. When her mother follows her instructions, her lower lip relaxes. Pointing is a way of calling your attention to an object. It is more specific than crying or gazing and is a step toward words. You can name what's pointed to before getting it. Later you can pretend you don't know which item your baby wants unless she names it.

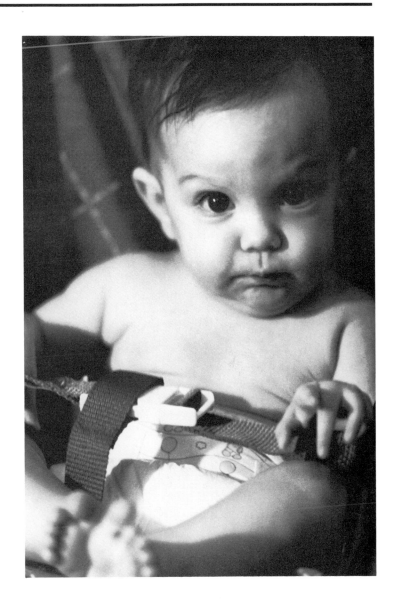

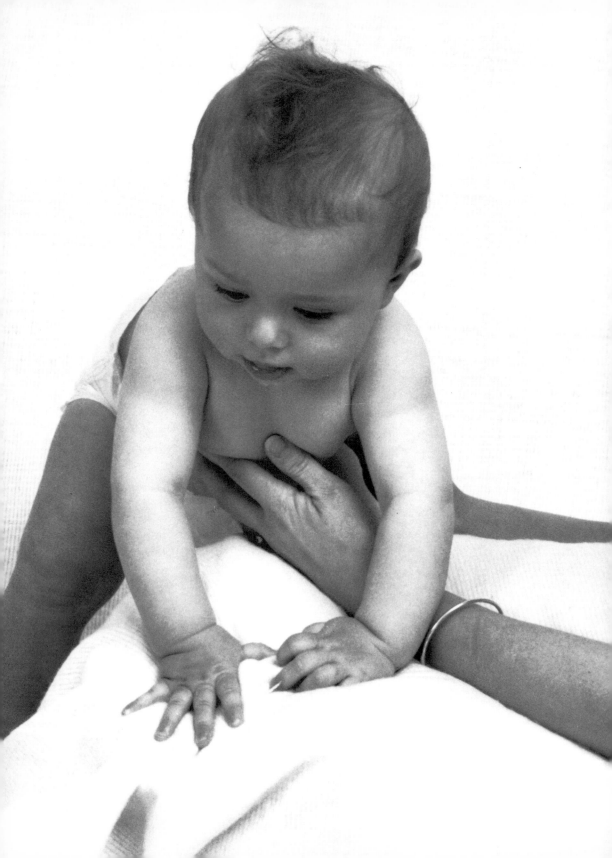

Seven to Twelve Months

Between the seventh and twelfth month, your infant realizes the separateness of others. Sometimes she enjoys this sensation, sometimes she feels threatened because she is also becoming more attached to you. The concept of "we" takes root, and the baby learns that "both of us" can share an experience. Now your baby looks to you for reassurance or approval. To get your attention, she may point, whine, smile, or mug.

New emotions during these months include boredom, petulance, shame, confidence, and wariness. Wariness, a mixture of fear and interest, is especially important because it will help keep your new crawler safe. A wary baby will hesitate while she figures out a situation. Some parents misinterpret wariness as shyness to be overcome with a push or a "come on, now." This will only make the baby less secure. She needs to case the locale or person at her own speed. Some infants rush ahead before thinking and so are prone to accidents. Others hold back too much and miss all the fun. Your mutual signaling system will soften these extremes.

Wariness is an example of an emotional blend, the mixing or telescoping of two emotions that previously happened one after the other. Blends show that your baby is having more complex feelings. As the first birthday approaches, you'll see such blends as smiling mixed with fear—you may think she's being insincere, but she's actually trying to reassure herself. Flirting is one blend of "come here/go away." Your baby may signal "no" but coyly ask to be coaxed.

The meaning of "no" cues changes. Previously, a "no" meant "stop it," "change something," or "leave me alone." Now it might mean, "I don't like what's happening" or "give me time to figure this out." After twelve months, "no" signals sometimes mean "let me do it my way" or "unless I thought of it first, I'm not doing it, so don't make any suggestions."

By nine months, your baby has learned to play with face muscles. For example, she'll raise her eyebrows to ask a question, wrinkle her nose to be flirtatious, or make faces to be funny or friendly.

By one year, your baby's ability to communicate will have come a long way from the early signals to approach or avoid. Together you will have developed a mutually satisfactory signaling system. You will have built the foundation upon which your toddler will learn to understand and speak language. And by tuning in to your baby's signals, you will have taken a fascinating journey with your baby through the most eventful year of her life.

The raised eyebrows are asking, "Is this all right?" About nine months, your baby will start looking to you to share his discoveries, to comfort him, or to reassure him. Nine-month-old Eric wants to know whether it's okay that the toy has come apart. His eyelids and parted lips show that he's relaxed—he's just looking for the all clear signal.

Nicole, who's one year old, is uncertain. Her mouth turns down, her eyes are open wide so that the whites show, and her head is averted. She's looking at her mother for reassurance. When your baby starts "referencing" you this way, you've reached an exciting new state in communicating together.

Nicole passes from wariness to surprise,
to fear, to seeking information from her
mother, who is on hand to offer reassurance.
With Mother's help, she makes a speedy
recovery. ▷▷▷

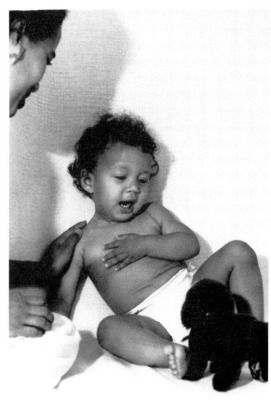

"Something interesting is about to happen."

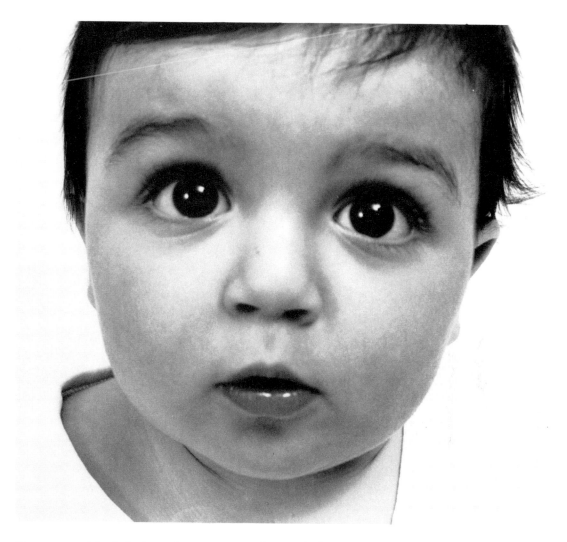

Because an older baby has a longer memory, he can feel not
only interest but expectancy. Based on his previous experiences,
David expects that something interesting is coming up. His
head leans forward, and his brows are questioning. His eyes
are wide open but not tense. His lips are relaxed and slightly
open. He's full of anticipation.

"I want to get to know that doggie."

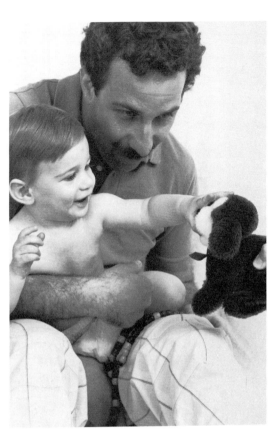

After trying several toys, Alex's father makes a great hit with this dog. The ten-month-old immediately throws up his arms and opens his hands as if to grasp it. His bright smile shows that he expects to like the dog. His father wisely leaves the dog where it is, letting Alex reach out to explore it rather than thrusting it in his face. Alex gets a good grip on the dog and reaches his head down to explore it. By letting Alex satisfy his curiosity and by not imposing his adult reactions, Alex's father is helping him build confidence through exploration. It is easy to support an infant's drive to discover and find fascination in the world around him.

"Ho hum."

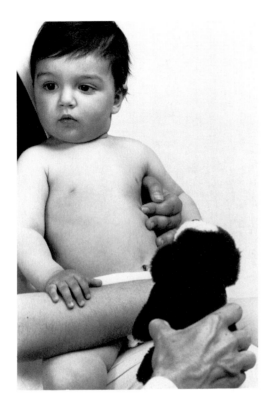

Boredom is a new mood that you'll start to see after nine months. These babies' eyes are dull and stare into space. They look drowsy and detached. Their cheeks and even their torsos are limp. If your child looks bored, wait and see if he can climb out of the mood himself. After a few minutes, you might suggest an activity or two.

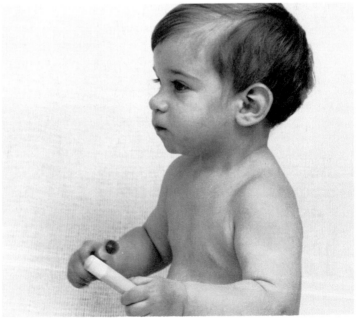

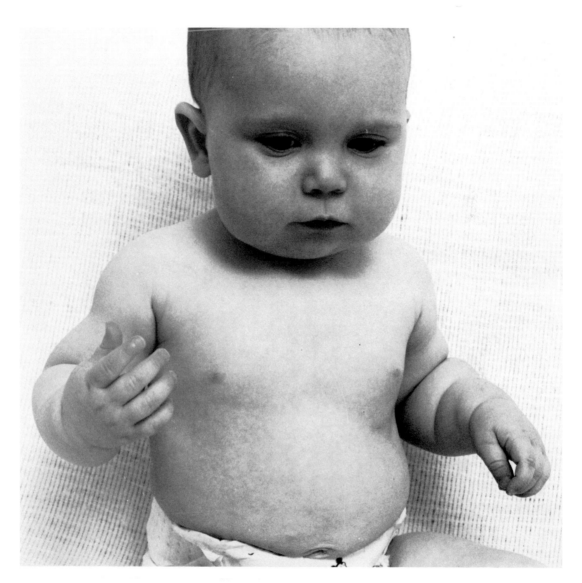

Seven-month-old Zoe is on the edge of boredom. As she quietly regards a toy, she appears drowsy and her eyes are dull. The right hand expresses some interest, but the left hand doesn't. This is a baby in suspended animation.

"That looks suspicious."

After six months, your baby may start to be suspicious of unfamiliar objects and people. She will hesitate, giving herself time to figure them out. Seven-month-old Zoe's hands show her mixed feelings—the right hand is getting ready to reach for the toy, while the left hand is avoiding it. There is wariness in her furrowed brow and loosened lower lip.

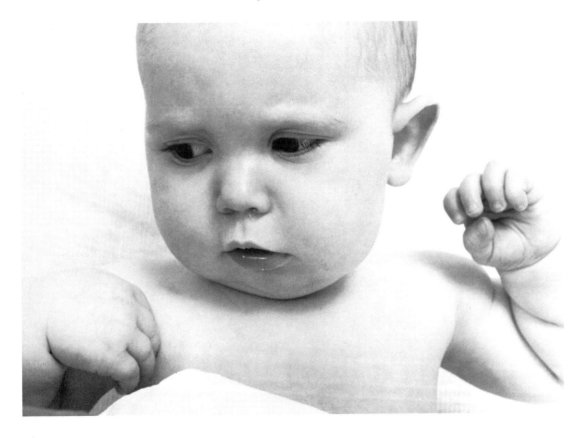

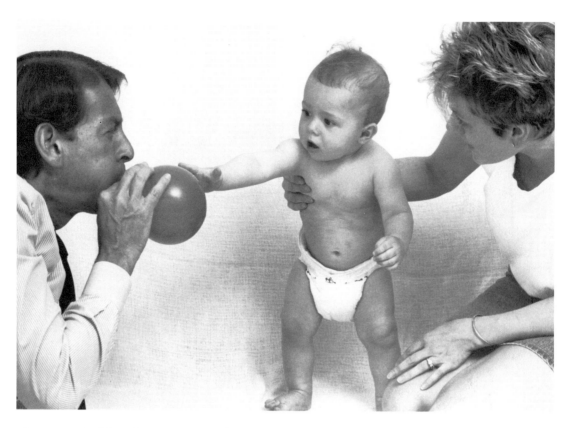

Eleven-month-old Stephen's interest in the balloon, shown
by his stretched-out right arm, is overcoming his wariness,
although his brow is still knit and the left arm is holding
back. When your baby looks wary, give him time to sort out
his feelings.

"Do I like this monkey?"

David isn't sure he likes the monkey until his mother convinces him it's nice. His initial wariness is shown by his averted eyes, raised brows, stretched and skeptical upper lip, and downturned mouth corners.

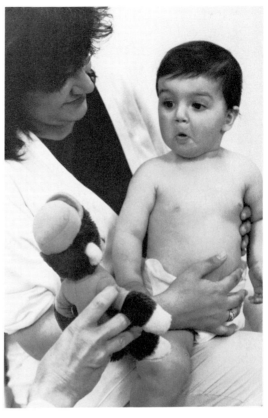

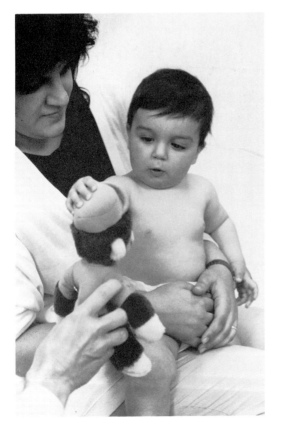

When he decides it's okay to reach out and touch the toy, his face relaxes, especially the brows, lips, and eyelids. He has a faint smile. Gentle encouragement by talking, smiling, and animating the toy will help to build his confidence.

"I'm feeling shy."

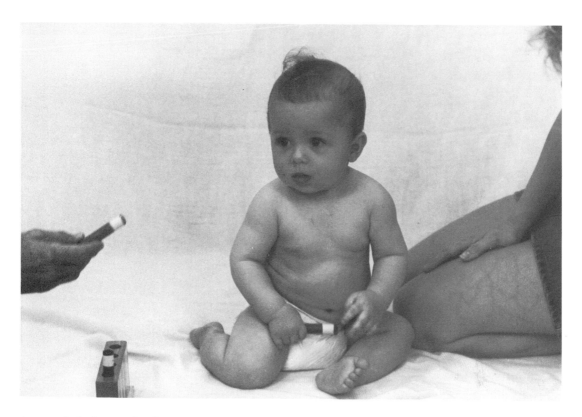

As your baby learns that he is a separate person at six or
seven months, he may show his first signs of shyness around
unfamiliar people. When I offered a toy to Stephen, he seemed
to draw up inside himself. By turning his body away, pulling
in his chin, and sticking out his tongue and lower lip, he's saying
he doesn't want to get involved. Other babies show their shyness
by averting their eyes and lowering their heads. Stephen's mother
can help him get over his shyness by taking the toy, getting
him interested in it, then handing it back to the stranger. The
stranger can then try offering it to him again. If your baby
is feeling shy, you can help by playing with the stranger yourself,
say by rolling a ball back and forth or offering him beads
to string. Strangers must move slowly and not move too close
too quickly to the infant. They should let the baby approach
them.

"How disappointing."

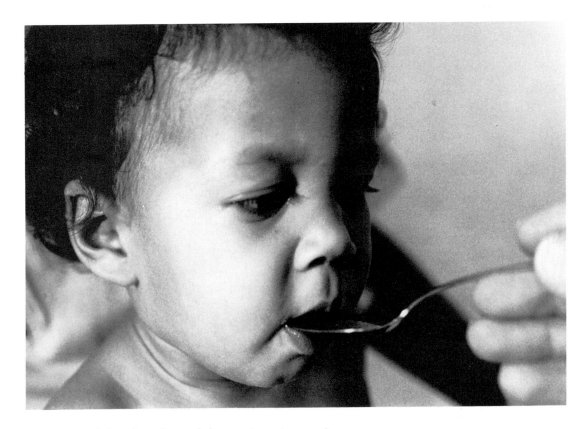

By one year, babies have learned that wariness is sometimes
well justified, because it can end in disappointment. Nicole's knit
brow shows that she's skeptical of what's on the spoon.

When it turns out to be something she doesn't like, those brows turn more sharply down. She frowns, sticking out her lower lip and wrinkling her nose in disgust.

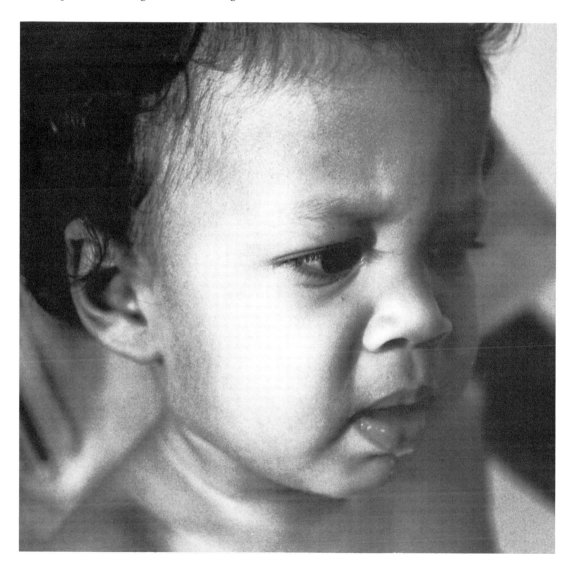

"I'm in a bad mood. Will someone help me out?"

Nine-month-old Natalie is being petulant, a complex mood that starts during these months. It is shown by a turned down mouth, turned up eyebrows, and sagging cheeks. Also called peevishness, it is composed partly of disgust, as seen by her wrinkled nose and raised lower lip, and partly by angry discontent as shown by her tight fists. Petulance is almost impossible to miss or ignore, because it's usually accompanied by an annoying whine.

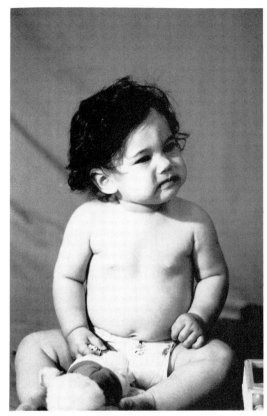

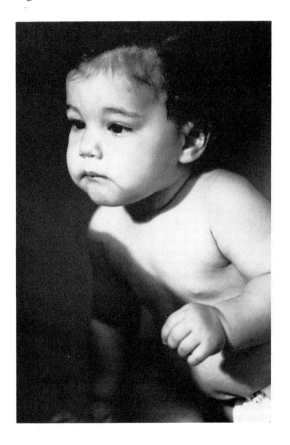

When Natalie's ill humor is ignored, it turns into fussy anger; she demands her mother's attention by shouting, reaching out, and throwing back her head. She is ready for a diversion or a companion in misery. No parent likes petulance—but it may help you to know that your baby is only asking for attention from her favorite person, you. One way to effectively help your infant when in this condition is to join her by means of role-playing. Show a puppet being peevish, and then make up a story to show how the puppet overcomes its misery.

"I'm feeling peevish."

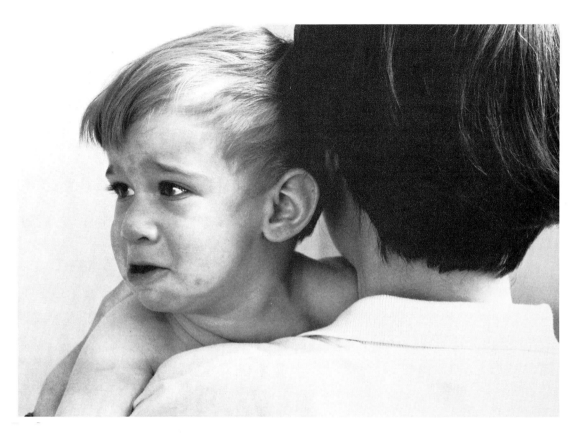

Here are two more babies in a petulant mood. On Alex's face are the classic signs of turned up brows, turned down mouth, and sagging cheeks. That lower lip is starting to quiver, too.

Nicole shows another sign of petulance—squirming. She's shouting and grimacing, too. Trying to be calm in the face of this mood does help in part. Trying to distract the baby won't be helpful. Letting your baby watch while you solve your own petulance is the best way. By showing good humor when you're disappointed, concentrating on the positive while admitting that you're peeved, you'll show the path toward acceptable behavior.

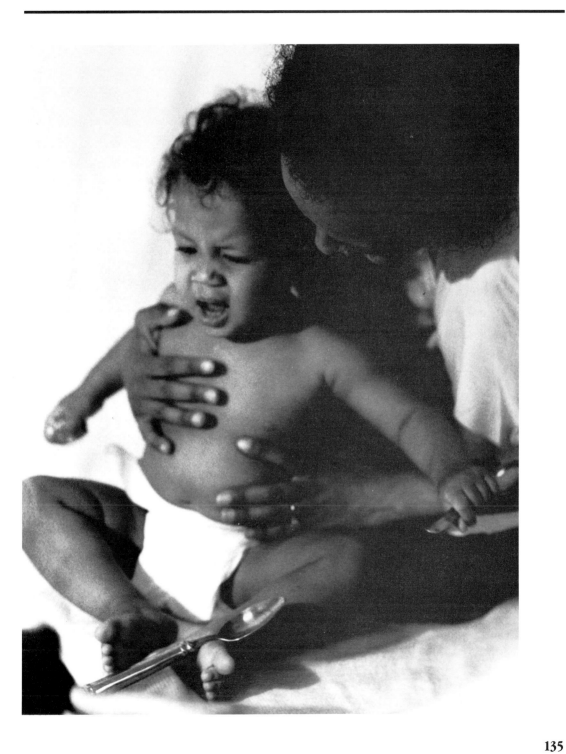

"I can't deal with all this jumping and barking."

Zoe is wary of the dog from the start, and when it suddenly barks and flips, she sneezes to shut herself quickly off from the noise and action. She pulls back her shoulders, too. Older babies continue to send the same disengagement cues as younger infants, but now they often need to step back for just a moment rather than shut down completely.

"But I don't want to hug you right now."

Eric's father is looking for a hug. At first, the nine-month-old just looks disinterested; his face is neutral and sober. But his brows are starting to draw together, signaling aversion.

Then he actually pushes himself away, a strong sign that he wants no part of this.

Disengagement cues become more adult-like as babies get older. Natalie shakes her head "no" and dramatically scissors her arms to block the spoon. Other "stop" signs are the clenched mouth, lowered head, and sagging cheeks. Around nine months, most babies start to say "no" by shaking their heads and pursing their lips tightly. This cue is partly saying "stop it, I don't want it." Partly, however, it is saying "give me space and time to do it my own way." When your child says "no," you can take the attitude "I didn't know you had your own ideas on this—show me and perhaps I can do it your way." If you are able to agree with your baby, you can then say, "This time I did what you wanted, next time maybe you'll do it my way; we can take turns." You can start taking this attitude now, and your child will come to understand the words over the next years.

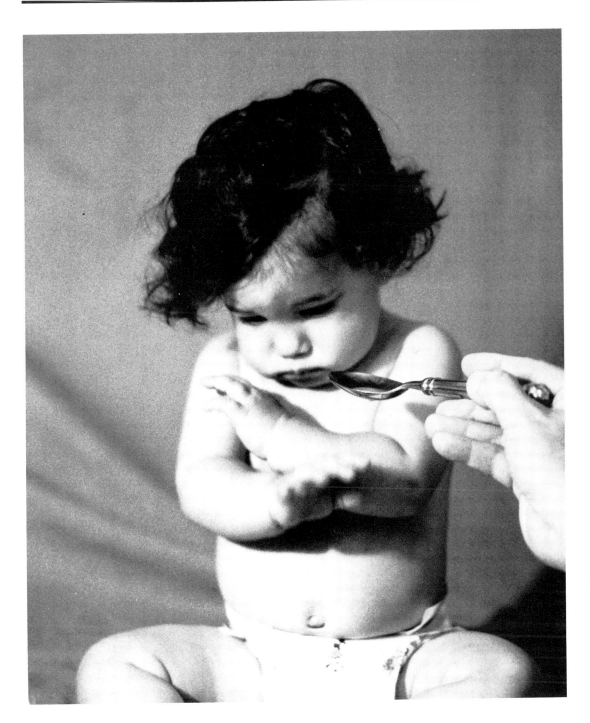

"Now you've made me mad."

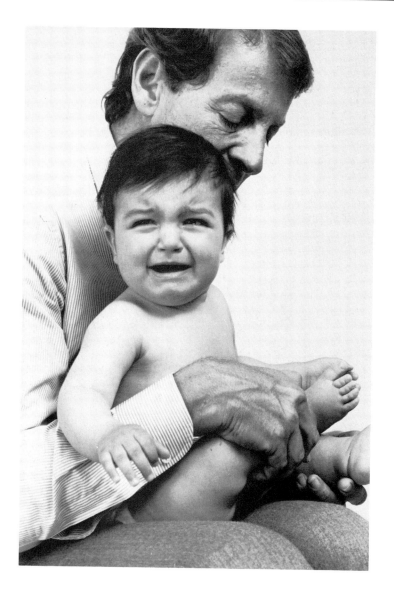

Drawn-together brows show that these babies are angry. When I try to hold David's foot, he turns his eyes and head away.

Natalie is hunching her shoulders and wrinkling her nose. Infants often have a legitimate reason to be discontent, but we adults may not have figured it out. Instead of causing further insult by criticizing the infant's anger or saying "shush," we would do better to try to figure out what happened.

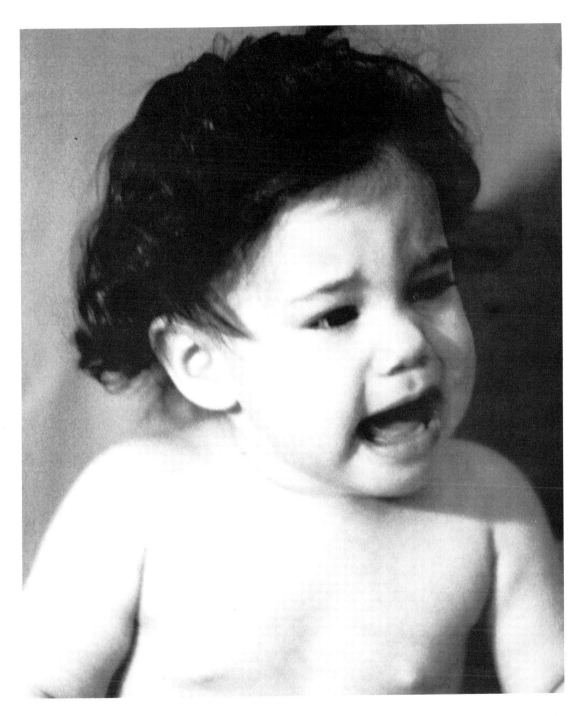

"I'm scared—take it easy!"

In roughhousing, the happiness is mixed
with fear. The line between them is easy to
cross. Alex's arched back is a potent cue
of fear, as are the withdrawn arms, apprehen-
sively raised brows, and closing fingers.

When he's hoisted overhead, he laughs. But
in the next instant play goes too far and
he's afraid. The smile ebbs, his brows knit,
and he's about to cry. Be on the lookout
for fear mixed with the giggles of your baby
during rough play.

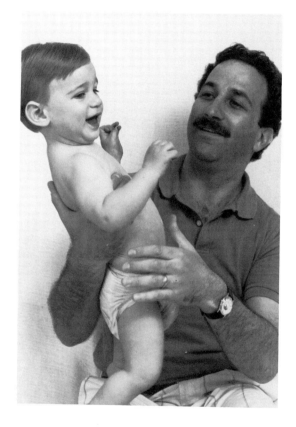

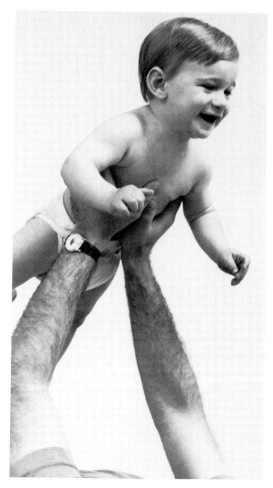

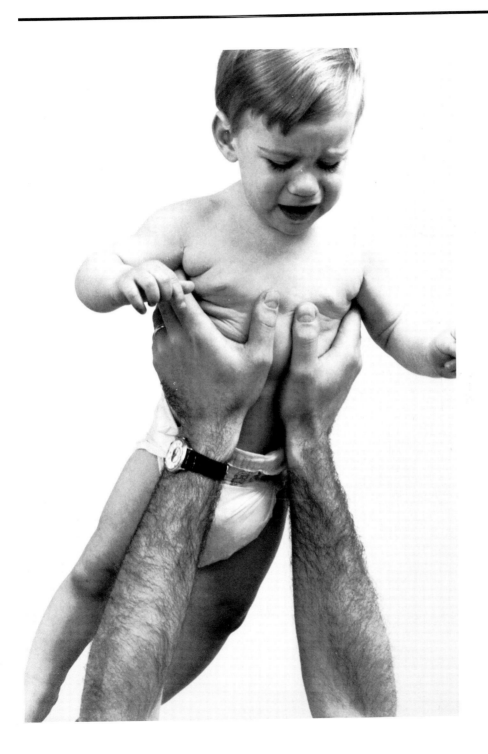

Nicole spreads out her arms in fear. The stiff body, whites
of her eyes, and lowered brows show she's afraid to be perched
on the horse. Her tongue shows her aversion. Yet her face
is sober, not panicky, as she looks for her mother's signals
to tell her she's okay. During these months, the mood of fear
is expanded into worry as the baby becomes able to remember
being scared. Her parents can try borrowing a lower or safer
rocking toy to get Nicole used to the sensation. Turning worry
into confidence is a particular pleasure for parents.

"Hey, Mom, look at me."

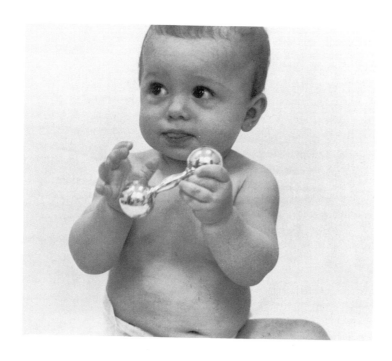

Another new mood your baby will show is coyness— a reluctance to make a definite commitment until you give your approval. It's clearly okay to like a rattle, but Stephen sticks out his tongue in mock dislike and looks for encouragement.

To get her mother's attention, Zoe pretends something's wrong by sticking out her tongue and lower lip.

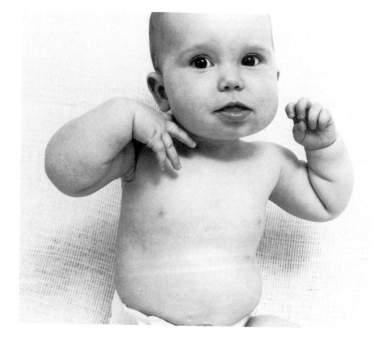

A sucked-in lower lip usually shows dislike. But Nicole's bright, happy face shows that she's doing it for her mother's benefit, so she'll encourage her to play with the blocks. The one-year-old is playing a trick. Increasingly, babies become able to use their facial expressions consciously in mugging and mockery.

"I'm just showing off."

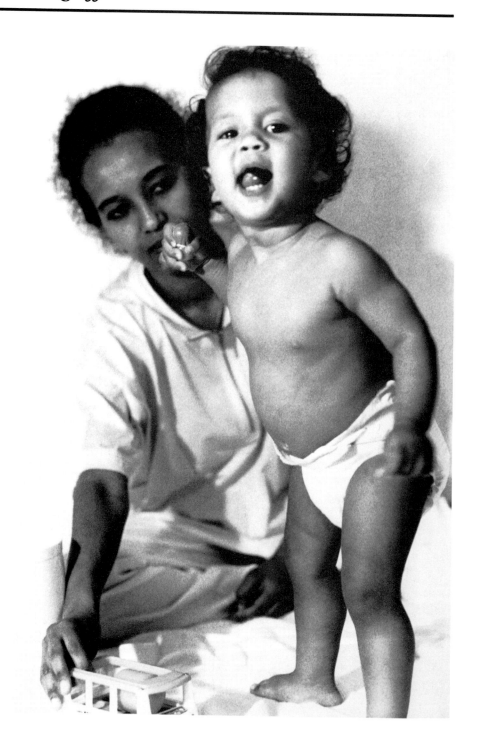

You'll sometimes discover your older baby showing off for you, just as these babies did for our camera. Both babies are relaxed and smiling as they unselfconsciously clown around. Nicole takes a break from playing with her mother to show off her tongue.

Stephen gives a shout of pleasure as he exuberantly shows himself to the camera.

"Applause, please."

Nicole is affecting exagge-rated signs of happiness to get attention. First she opens her mouth in a too-wide smile. Then she coyly throws back her head and shows off her teeth. She's clearly just as interested in how her mother will respond as in enjoying herself. The old-est of our babies, Nicole is able to have one emotion and pretend another—toddlers are capable of theatrics.

"That looks like fun."

During the first year, babies don't really play together. But they do notice and copy each other. One baby explores and likes the dog, so the other thinks he'd better check it out, too. Both babies are relaxed and open to new experiences. Except when struggling with each other or for a toy the other has, babies enjoy being near peers. Other babies offer interesting spectacles that suggest activities. In the early months, if one baby cries loudly, another may think he's already crying himself, and start to cry, too. There's something less threatening about being near someone as small as you. On the other hand, the "other" is not trying to attune himself with you. This can be distressing and frustrating. Watch your baby in the company of others. He may get along with one peer but not another.

Zoe's face radiates happiness as she looks into her mother's eyes. She's relaxed from her eyebrows to her flopped-open feet.

Stephen's strongly focused, happy eyes and uplifted head show he's open for love. When you understand your baby's talk and your baby is able to read your messages, those connections will reward you many times over.

The Arrival Times of
Your Baby's Expressions

These are the average, approximate times when you can look for each facial expression; your baby may first show these expressions earlier or later.

PRESENT AT BIRTH:
Interested
Distressed
Startled

FOUR TO EIGHT WEEKS:
Smiling

THREE TO FOUR MONTHS:
Surprised
Enraged
Pleased

FIVE TO NINE MONTHS:
Disgusted
Angry
Afraid
Sad
Avoiding
Curious
Joyful
Wary

NINE TO TWELVE MONTHS:
Repulsed
Petulant
Anticipating
Bored
Coy
Anxious
Confident
Elated

About the Author

Sirgay Sanger, M.D. is the founder and director of the Early Care Center in New York City, the first private facility in the nation devoted exclusively to the emotional and social well-being of healthy infants and families. Dr. Sanger also founded the Parent/Child Interaction Program at St. Luke's-Roosevelt Hospital in New York.

A graduate of the Harvard Medical School, Dr. Sanger completed his postgraduate work at Columbia University Psychoanalytic Clinic. He is the author of *You and Your Baby's First Year*; *The Woman Who Works, the Parent Who Cares*; and *Emotional Care of Hospitalized Children*.